WHAT PEO[PLE ARE SAYING ABOUT DOUG]
STRINGE[R]

The ministry of Somebody Cares and Doug Stringer exemplify the command found in the Good Samaritan story. Obeying this teaching of Jesus, they have gone and continue to "go and do likewise." We are thankful for their servant leadership and for the example they set in doing the Word. We have seen it firsthand and are honored to partner with them.

—*Larry and Leah Ramirez*
Founders, Ask for the Nations

Doug Stringer knows what works, for the Lord has given him a blueprint that is transforming the fourth largest city in America and is spreading across the country and the globe. It's time for a marriage of heart commitment to Jesus with the fulfillment found in unity and servanthood. Doug embodies both, and he shares how it can happen to you and your church, too.

—*Ché Ahn*
Senior pastor, Harvest Rock Church, Pasadena, CA

Somebody Cares and the ministries associated with it have been and are impacting communities around the globe. Doug Stringer and the ministries he helps to serve and steward have uniquely been able to connect and interface with all the primary movements in the church today. When I think of Doug's decades of ministry, I see the consistency of: 1) intimacy with Jesus; 2) justice in society; 3) compassion for people through good works; 4) continual prayer; 5) evangelism and/or revival; 6) unity with honor of the body of Christ; and 7) revival of character in leadership and integrity with humility in personal character. The world needs the manifest presence of the Lord and to see the tangibility of His presence. The message of a passion for God and a compassion for souls is exemplified through the life and message you will find in *Mending the Net: Bringing Hope in a Hurting World* by Doug Stringer.

—*Mike Bickle*
International House of Prayer, Kansas City

I have watched Doug over the years literally model the things that are written in this book. Jesus is his model of humility and servitude. His understanding of the life of Christ as a servant, healer, reconciler, and deliverer has made its indelible mark upon the pages of *Mending the Net*. Read it and it will make its mark upon your heart. This book will help you to move from trying to practice what you preach to preaching what you practice. It's time to manifest the kingdom. This book will help you do just that. If you need practical tools to help you meet felt needs through humility and servitude, watch Doug's life and read this book. You won't find a contradiction. Doug is somebody who cares.

—*Bishop Vaughn McLaughlin*
Senior pastor, The Potter's House International Ministries
CEO, Kingdom Plaza Mall

Doug Stringer was a city reacher before city reaching was cool. His book tells what happens when the church is obedient to carry our heavenly Father's heart for our city. If you are ready to do the will of the Father in your city, you need this book.

—*Daniel Bernard*
Executive director, Somebody Cares Tampa Bay, FL

This book contains not only the heart of Doug Stringer but also the heart of the Father for the lost. In this hour, when hopelessness and despair are spread through every avenue of media, this book is a good tonic. Somebody Cares doesn't just point the way of hope, it *leads* the way. Read it and be inspired. Behave it and be blessed.

—*Walter Fletcher*
Fletchers Counseling, Dallas, TX

Somebody Cares is not just another evangelistic strategy. It is a reality in the life of Doug Stringer. His book clearly shows how the love of Christ is the only hope we have to make a difference in our cities in this generation. If you want to be a part of something bigger than yourself, if you want to make a difference in this world, you need to read this book. It will change your life!

—*Roger L. Helle*
President, Roger Helle Ministries, Chattanooga, TN
Retired executive director, Teen Challenge of the Mid-South

In 2012, Somebody Cares and Eden Counseling and Consulting worked closely together to provide support and training to churches after Hurricane Sandy. We have spoken together in several venues since then and Doug has earned my respect and admiration. Doug is very consistently excellent. He speaks, manages, directs, and writes with grace, expertise, and professionalism. He is a great communicator. Doug probably has no idea of the impact he has had on my life and ministry. We interact a few times a year, but he always says something that hits home.

The stories in *Mending the Net* are inspiring. This book is very important in the context of our current cultural crises. As Doug says in chapter 3, "Each individual, church, or ministry, working together and doing their part, can impact a whole city with the gospel."

He calls us to unite to serve our Lord and our local communities. This is the gospel in action. Doug provides biblical grounding, sound theology, and a track record of results that prove that diverse groups of people can work together when they focus on Christ instead of our differences. Doug has been uniting people for a long time and I know that you will gain insight from *Mending the Net* into what God wants you to do within your sphere of relationships.

—*Paul VanValin, Ph.D.*
Founder, Eden Leaders Institute
VanValin Assessment & Consulting

Doug Stringer lives and writes with an amazing combination of humility and passion. He is not writing from an ivory tower about a theory that sounds good but has no practical relevance. Doug has fought the battles in the trenches. He has sown his life into the lives of men and women from every ethnic and denominational back- ground in the city. The result? God is uniting His church in Houston, and revival is underway.

—*Jim Herrington*
The Leader's Journey
Former executive director, Mission Houston

Doug Stringer has become a leading instrument of harvest in the city of Houston, with a ripple effect reaching out into America and other nations. The heartbeat of his ministry points to the very heart and intentions of God that none should perish.

—*Scott Hinkle*
Founder, Scott Hinkle Outreach Ministries

From prayer warriors to church leaders, all will be challenged by Doug Stringer's revelation of God's purpose to fulfill the destiny of the church. His experience and revelation should be required reading in every school of ministry.

—*John P. Kelly*
Founder, International Coalition of Apostolic Leaders

As a member of the Houston media, I believe it is very import- ant for the body of Christ to be well-informed of the workings of the Holy Spirit through God's people. Somebody Cares Houston provides such a vehicle through the dedicated leadership of Doug Stringer, one of the greatest proponents of Christ-centered unity in our generation. Somebody Cares is a powerful tool in the hands of Almighty God.

—*Kimberly Kossie-McKee*
Former community relations director, KSBJ Radio
Senior pastor, Latter Day Deliverance Revival Church, Houston

Lakewood Church is proud to be part of the Somebody Cares network. Our desire is to cross all denominational, racial, and economic lines in an effort to changes lives, and this book is a textbook of how this is done. Want to change your community? Start acting on the principles in this remarkable book.

—*Joel Osteen*
Pastor, Lakewood Church, Houston, TX

Doug Stringer understands the correlation between prayer, worship, reconciliation, mercy, ministry, and evangelism as few men I know. He literally does the stuff required by God in Isaiah 58 for the healing of a land. Reading his book is like encountering a flame—it will either enlighten and inspire you, or burn you with shame and conviction, depending on how it finds you.

—*Jimmy Owens*
Author, *Heal Our Land: Steps to Saving Our Nation*

The ministry of Somebody Cares is being lived out in Houston, Texas. God has used Doug Stringer to help the church see that, together, we can get our arms around a city of any size. Underneath Doug's gentle, humble spirit is a passion for revival that challenges all who hear him to examine their lives and move into all God has for them.

—*Steve Riggle*
President, Grace International
Senior pastor, Grace Church at the Woodlands

This book is absolutely a must-read for those who wish to see their city transformed. Doug Stringer speaks with the authority and credibility of someone who lives daily the principles of love and compassion for the needy. Read this book. It will change you for the better.

—*Ed Silvoso*
President, Harvest Evangelism, San Jose, CA

The message of Somebody Cares is the rallying cry of the Holy Spirit to the bride of Christ today. Doug Stringer is God's mouthpiece to impart this very timely message to the fragmented body of Christ. The message of the "mended net" should convict all of us to tear apart the barriers that we have built around our churches for so long. Do you want to reap a great harvest of souls? If so, *hear what the Spirit says to the churches!*

—Paul Tan
Senior pastor, City Blessing Churches

The spiritual wilderness is crying out for a voice. Doug Stringer is that voice, offering new hope and a vision for reaching the lost that is practical and easily implemented in Houston and cities around the world.

—Terry Tekyl
Renewal Ministries, Spring, TX

Doug Stringer communicates the heart of our Father to church leaders, to the classroom setting, and to gang leaders alike. He shares a message of functional unity that is demonstrated through the networking of ministers in both our local communities and our international megachurches.

—Dr. Joseph Umidi
Executive vice president for student life, Regent University

MENDING
THE
NET

MENDING THE NET

BRINGING HOPE IN A HURTING WORLD

FOUNDER OF SOMEBODY CARES

DOUG STRINGER

W

WHITAKER
HOUSE

MENDING THE NET
Bringing Hope in a Hurting World

Somebody Cares International
P.O. Box 925308
Houston, TX 77292
www.somebodycares.org
www.dougstringer.com

ISBN: 978-1-64123-608-9
eBook ISBN: 978-1-64123-609-6
Printed in the United States of America
© 2021 by Doug Stringer

Whitaker House
1030 Hunt Valley Circle
New Kensington, PA 15068
www.whitakerhouse.com

Library of Congress Cataloging-in-Publication Data (Pending)

1 2 3 4 5 6 7 8 9 10 11   ᵾᵾ   28 27 26 25 24 23 22 21

DEDICATION

I dedicate this book to my heroes of the faith. With a passion for God and a compassion for souls, you are true witnesses who rescue lives. Over the past twenty years, you have taken the DNA of this ministry from the streets of Houston, Texas, to the four corners of the world.

I am so grateful for my staff, who stand with me in the vision. You are the *team* the Lord has raised up in this hour.

To my spiritual family, it is an honor to serve you as you serve Christ.

In loving memory of those who have gone to be with the Lord: John, Mark, Bill, Brandy, Isaiah, and Johnny. They overcame physical death by AIDS to gain eternity with Christ.

To all of you unknown soldiers who are sowing your lives for the gospel. May the Lord of the harvest grant your heart's cry for spiritual awakening across the land. Together may we see with our eyes what our hearts have longed for—souls saved, lives changed, and revival. As the prophet Eli spoke to Hannah, *"Go in peace, and the God of Israel grant your petition which you have asked of Him"* (1 Samuel 1:17).

CONTENTS

FOREWORD

It was the midpoint in a two-session pastors' gathering in Houston. I was the speaker and had just concluded my cup-of-tea standard for the *coffee break* in such a setting. When the emcee reassembled the more than 300 pastors who were present, I thought he was about to call me back when, instead, he asked a clear-eyed young man with a pleasant demeanor to make an announcement.

As it turned out, the announcement was about fifteen minutes long—but no one in the room disapproved, and neither did I. First, because they knew—everyone in the room knew—that what was being shared was more than simply, "Hey, here's what's comin' up (if you happen to care)." The announcement was detailed and the interest level was high because virtually everyone there was connected to what the young leader was talking about.

That's when I first met Doug Stringer.

It was a discovery of the first magnitude. As I listened, I turned to my host and whispered, "Who is this guy? He's got it!"

Here's just a smattering of what I learned.

Doug Stringer is the driving dynamic behind Somebody Cares, Houston. Under the touch of the Spirit of God, he has moved into an arena of divinely given influence to unite hundreds of congregations in that city and bring about immensely wonderful and awesomely powerful things... as God views *powerful*.

Doug Stringer is also a servant, surrendered to the spirit of sacrificial self-giving in order to answer God's call. With no guaranteed salary, he not only sold his own possessions to launch into the citywide cause he seeks to serve, but he also requires no guarantee of income to continue. Crisp and sharp in his appearance, sensitive and fluent in his communication, the last thing you would expect is a person ready to answer something like an ancient oath of poverty for the sake of ministry. Of course, that isn't exactly what Doug has done, but the spirit of such abandonment to faith for the sake of greater fruitfulness is at the root of his commitment.

Not only is Doug Stringer a voice for unity, but he also issues a clarion call that *the giants in the land* of today's cities can be conquered for the glory of God. I was moved by the visible evidence of even sometimes cynical pastors cooperating together because of this young man who is so stirred by God and so servant-hearted in his approach to leadership.

Doug Stringer is what I call a *city saint*. By that I mean he is a person like Abraham, who will intercede for a city's rescue from deserved judgment (Sodom); like Jeremiah, who will weep for a city's need and seek to call people to God's way in answering it (Jerusalem); or like Joshua, who will see the obstacle blocking a city's future and mobilize people to unite and march together until God's power changes it (Jericho).

There is a call today for city saints—for people of God who will capture a sense of His heart for their city and *live it out*.

City saints aren't spiritual gurus or people accomplished at religious exercises. They are simply willing vessels whose hearts are captivated by two things: the cry of their city's need and the possibilities of God's people making a difference.

City saints see beyond the problems and the pain of their urban environment and see the hand of God reaching out with promise *if* His people will join hands with that promise found in Jeremiah 29:7:

> *Seek the peace of the city where I have caused you to [come], and pray to the LORD for it; for in its peace you will have peace.*

All of us live someplace where there is a cry for people who will love the needy and band together to serve them. Doug Stringer has something to say about how that can happen—anywhere, with anyone, in any church or in any town. He is a proven city saint who doesn't think anything more of himself than that he's simply your brother in Christ.

That's the best kind.

Take a couple hours and discover more of what I suddenly found in those few moments at the pastors' gathering. It will make your day and might even result in remaking your city.

—*Jack W. Hayford*
Founding pastor, The Church on the Way
Chancellor emeritus, The King's University, Van Nuys, CA

PREFACE

THE PARABLE OF
THE FISHLESS FISHERMEN

A story has been told that is a good illustration of where we, the church, often find ourselves today. It is the story of fishermen who lost sight of actually catching fish.

There was once a group called the Fishermen's Fellowship. They were surrounded by streams and lakes full of hungry fish and met regularly to discuss the call to fish, the abundance of fish, and the thrill of catching fish. The more they talked, the more excited they got about fishing.

Someone suggested they needed a philosophy of fishing, so they carefully defined and redefined the art and purpose of fishing. They developed elaborate fishing strategies and tactics and felt a smug satisfaction in the progress they were making toward their calling as fishermen.

One day, they realized they had been going about it backwards. They had approached fishing from the point of view of the fisherman and not from the point of view of the fish. How do fish view the world? How do fishermen appear to fish? What do fish eat and when? They agreed that these are all good things to know, so they devoted themselves to researching the habits of fish and attended numerous helpful conferences on fishing. Some traveled to faraway places to study the characteristics of different kinds of fish; one even got a Ph.D. in fishology. But no one had yet gone fishing.

So a committee was formed to send out fishermen. Since the prospective fishing places outnumbered the available fishermen, the committee needed to determine priorities. A priority list of fishing places was posted on bulletin boards in all of the group's fellowship halls. But still, no one was fishing. A survey was launched to find out why. Most did not answer the survey, but from those who did, it was discovered that some felt called to study fish, a few to furnish fishing equipment, and several to go around encouraging the fishermen. However, with all their meetings, conferences, and committees, they simply didn't have time to fish.

Now Jake was a newcomer to the Fishermen's Fellowship. After one particularly stirring meeting, Jake decided to actually go fishing. He tried some of the techniques he had heard about, got the hang of it, and caught a choice fish.

At the next meeting, Jake told his story and the other fishermen were thrilled by his success. They honored him for his catch and enthusiastically scheduled him to speak at all the other fellowship chapters and explain how he did it. Because of all the speaking invitations and his election to the board of directors of the Fishermen's Fellowship, Jake no longer had time to go fishing.

Soon, however, Jake began to feel restless and unfulfilled. He longed to feel the tug on the line once again. So he cut his busy speaking schedule, resigned from the board, and said to a friend, "Let's go fishing!" They did, just the two of them, and they caught fish. The members of the Fishermen's Fellowship were many and the fish were plentiful, but the fishers were few!

PART OF THE NET

If you want a degree in fishology, don't read this book. But if you want to go out and fish, this book is for you. And take a partner—there is too much work to be done to fish with only one pole.

When Jesus first called the disciples, He called them to be fishers of men. Jesus told them to cast their net on the other side of the boat. As soon as they obeyed, they caught so many fish, the net was about to break. They signaled to their partners in the other boat to come help them. (See Luke 5:1–11.) It is the same for us; we need each other. In fact, we cannot do this great work alone.

After Jesus's death and resurrection, Peter went back to what he knew how to do—catching fish. (See John 21.) Jesus appeared to him at the Sea of Galilee and again instructed him and the other disciples with him to cast the net on the other side of the boat. They made a phenomenally large catch, yet their net did not break.

Each of us represents just one part of the net. Only by working together can we fulfill Christ's Great Commission to make disciples of all nations.

When we work together as the body of Christ, we can have that same testimony. Each of us represents just one part of the net.

Only by working together can we fulfill Christ's Great Commission to make disciples of all nations. (See Matthew 28:19–20.) The harvest will not come to its fullest extent without sacrifice and a servant's heart that says, "Whatever it takes, Lord. We will work together and get the job done."

It's all about souls—not about theories, competition, or doctrinal precision. It's about bringing lost people to Christ. It's about frontline participation in the harvest. This book is a true account of what God is doing to reach the lost through people working together. We have studied the principles of evangelism long enough—it's time to put them into action.

> *Multitudes upon multitudes are in the valley of decision between heaven and hell, and we have only a small window of time to reach them.*

What will it take to reach our cities? Multitudes upon multitudes are in the valley of decision between heaven and hell, and we have only a small window of time to reach them. Let's obey the Lord's command by fulfilling the Great Commission. He calls us to unite "*for such a time as this*" (Esther 4:14) to fulfill our purpose and meet our date with destiny. I pray that your heart is encouraged as you read this book and that you find your place as part of a net prepared to bring in a great harvest for God's kingdom.

ACKNOWLEDGMENTS

Special thanks to Jack Hayford for your friendship, mentorship, and support throughout the years and for being the one to first encourage me to write this book.

Thank you, Jim Buchan, for your contributions in editing. You took the original manuscript to the next level. Thanks so much for being a part of the team.

Joann Webster, I want to extend my gratitude for your heart of compassion that came through as you edited the original manuscript. You poured yourself into this project during a difficult season in your life. Your mother's legacy is exemplified through you.

Susie Wolf, thanks for your dedication and commitment to see the message get into people's hearts and hands.

Special thanks to Belinda Thacker, who has imbibed and carried the message of Somebody Cares. Thank you for your contributions to the ministry and to this book.

1

AUTHOR'S UPDATE 2021

> While men reach for thrones to build their own kingdoms, Jesus reached for a towel to wash men's feet. While we pursue exalted and high places, Jesus, the exalted One, left His highest place to pursue us.
> —Doug Stringer

If we're going to impact our generation in a world that's in turmoil and going through difficulties, we need to have a purpose greater than ourselves.

Scripture tells the story of when Saul had his Damascus road experience. Jesus gave him a revelation of Himself, and said, "I *have appeared to you for this purpose, to make you a minister and a witness both of the things which you have seen and of the things which I will yet reveal to you*" (Acts 26:16). In other words, the moment each and every one of us get a revelation of the work of the cross and the power of the resurrection, we have a purpose greater than ourselves. And that purpose is beyond building our own kingdom.

In the 1990s, the *Wall Street Journal* featured an article addressing businesses as they were trying to transition with the economy at the time. The headline read, "Collaborate or Die." In America right now, we see that while there are many churches that are growing, there are many others closing. Statistics say there are less people going to church now than there have been in the past. There is an alienation and a departure from the institutional church. It's important for us, then, to become part of a greater cause, to be a tangible expression of Christ to the world around us. The institutional church vs. the incarnational church is like religiosity vs. relationship. We need to be imitators of Christ rather than clones of modern-day religion.

In Luke 5, we find a very familiar area of Scripture:

When He had stopped speaking, He said to Simon, "Launch out into the deep and let down your nets for a catch." But Simon answered and said to Him, "Master, we have toiled all night and caught nothing; nevertheless at Your word I will let down the net." And when they had done this, they caught a great number of fish, and their net was breaking. So they signaled to their partners in the other boat to come and help them. And they came and filled both the boats, so that they began to sink. When Simon Peter saw it, he fell down at Jesus' knees, saying, "Depart from me, for I am a sinful man, O Lord!...And Jesus said to Simon, "Do not be afraid. From now on you will catch men."   (Luke 5:4–8, 10)

Now we know, of course, that for the next few years, Peter and the other disciples followed after Jesus. But something I noticed here in Luke and also in John 21 is that they *spread the net, washed the net, cast the net,* and *mended the net.* When we, too, as the body of Christ, are spread out together, washed together, mended together, and cast together, we catch a lot more fish. With one fishing pole, you catch only one fish at a time; but as a mended net, we bring a greater harvest of fish. In other words, we are able to do much more.

> When we, as the body of Christ, are spread out together, washed together, mended together, and cast together, we catch a lot more fish.

Notice here in this story that after they cast the net on the other side, they had to get their partners to help them because there were so many fish that the net was ripping open! Then Jesus said to follow Him and become fishers of men.

The principle here is this: the job that needs to be done out there is too big for any of us alone. We cannot do this alone. We need one another.

I like what Pastor Joe McKeever writes—and it can apply to any of us, not just to pastors:

The four-year-old who says, "I can do it by myself" has a lot in common with the typical pastor. Pastors are notorious for their lone ranger approach to ministry. It's what I call the number one failure of 90 percent of pastors. They prefer to go it alone.

The late Scottish pastor Robert McCheyne said, "There is nothing more deceitful than your estimate of your own strength."

Remember, you're not a tree that can stand alone. You're only a branch, and it's only when you abide in Christ that you will flourish.

Many times, under stress and tension, we go back to what we're comfortable doing rather than doing what God says to do. We see this happen with Peter and some of the other disciples after the crucifixion.

> *Simon Peter, Thomas called the Twin, Nathanael of Cana in Galilee, the sons of Zebedee, and two others of His disciples were together. Simon Peter said to them, "I am going fishing." They said to him, "We are going with you also." They went out and immediately got into the boat, and that night they caught nothing. But when the morning had now come, Jesus stood on the shore; yet the disciples did not know that it was Jesus. Then Jesus said to them, "Children, have you any food?" They answered Him, "No." And He said to them, "Cast the net on the right side of the boat, and you will find some." So they cast, and now they were not able to draw it in because of the multitude of fish.* (John 21:2–6)

This had to be a déjà vu moment for Peter! He was a professional fisherman, yet he wasn't able to catch the fish without the instruction from the Lord.

There are things that only Jesus can do in and through us that we can never do in our own strength or capacity. And through Christ, we need one another to get those things accomplished. It's a mended net working together, washed together, and cast together that brings in a greater harvest of fish.

> *There are things that only Jesus can do in and through us that we can never do in our own strength or capacity. And through Christ, we need one another to get those things accomplished.*

The Lord is still telling us today that the job to be done is bigger than any of us. We cannot do this as a lone ranger, using a fishing pole to pull in one fish. We need to become that mended net, part of a purpose and a cause greater than ourselves.

If we're going to make the kind of impact the Lord wants to make through us, there must be an exponential, synergistic move of God's presence upon the church and upon us, as leaders, to recognize we can't do this alone. We need one another. Otherwise, the net will rip open. We need each other if we're going to impact the generation and the nations in our time.

WHY MEND THE NET?

An earlier version of this book was published in 2001 under the title *Somebody Cares: a guide to living out your faith.* My original working title was *Mending the Net*, with the theme of *Passion for God, Compassion for Souls.* Promise Keepers distributed 1,000 copies of our prepublished version, entitled *Passion for God, Compassion for Souls.* You will find all three of these themes interconnected throughout this book.

We have returned to the original title because we believe that now, in our polarized culture that has even permeated parts of the church, it's more important than ever for us to cross our racial, denominational, and generational lines to be part of something bigger than ourselves. But it begins with a return to our greater purpose, which can only come from our knee posture with vertical worship. We need the presence and heart of the Lord to work in us and through us in tangible ways.

As we go to press, we have all seen and experienced a season full of challenges and uncertainties—from worldwide pandemics and pestilence that has led to economic challenges and sharp differences, to polarization and divisiveness, racial tensions, and even riots, lawlessness, and anarchy in some of our cities. Scriptures reveal to us that "all that can be shaken will be shaken" (see Hebrews 12:27), *"the whole creation groans and labors with birth pangs"* (Romans 8:22), and *"the nations rage"* (Psalm 2:1). Jesus mentions all of these and more in Luke 21, including the distress of nations with perplexity and men's hearts failing them from fear. More than ever, the church must be intentional about crossing our differences to bring healing and hope. Only a church united can bring healing and hope to a nation divided.

How do we do this?

+ First, we must *spread the net*, opening ourselves up in vulnerability before God.

+ Second, we must *wash the net*, as we allow God to cleanse us individually and corporately.

+ Third, we must *mend the net*, crossing our racial, generational, and denominational lines to be part of something bigger than ourselves.

+ And fourth, *cast the net*, as we allow God to cast us as a mended net together, to bring in a greater harvest.

There are many out there who are feeling weary in doing good, like they have nothing to give. But Jesus never asks us for what we don't have, only for what we do have. And when we offer what we have, with thanksgiving, he takes our fishes and loaves and multiplies them, giving us more than what we need.

> *When we offer what we have, with thanksgiving, Jesus takes our fishes and loaves and multiplies them, giving us more than what we need.*

It is my belief that, from a benevolence standpoint, the church in America has helped make America a blessing to the nations.

We have given to those who are suffering from disasters or hard times both in our own country and in other nations, regardless of their personal preferences, political persuasion, pigmentation, or religion. By caring for those in need, the church has given redemptive access to God's promise in Isaiah 58:8 that in our time of need for healing, our *"healing shall spring forth speedily."* This, I believe, is our redemptive thread as a nation.

CO-PASTORING A CITY

Although our ministry began in the early 1980s and was already involved across the nation and beyond, it was in 1995 that we launched a network called Somebody Cares Houston, unveiled as a citywide effort to reach out at a grassroots level to at-risk youth and those in low income urban communities. There was a need to link those working in struggling urban areas with suburban churches so the church in Houston could reach an entire city for Christ. I call this *co-pastoring a city.*

When you think in terms of pastoring a city with over six million people such as Houston, and beyond, you realize this is something you cannot do alone. You need to be part of something bigger than yourself. To quote a pastor from a local megachurch, "Doug has caused me to realize I am part of a team of shepherds, under the Great Shepherd, that is called to pastor a city of six million people."

Somebody Cares America/International has become known as a coalition and network of organizations and churches impacting communities through prayer initiatives, compassion outreaches, training and responding in times of crisis, as well as encouraging and equipping leaders globally. Together, we provide guidance to our chapters and centers, as well as partner churches, ministries, and organizations.

From Houston, Texas, to the four corners of the world, from urban to foreign missions, from inner cities to unreached people groups, we are impacting communities and helping to transform lives through united efforts of prayer, tangible expressions of Christ, and community transformation through kingdom collaborations. It is about the church serving communities and repairing the breach.

UNITED FOR A MONUMENTAL TASK

We have seen the critical importance of relationships to be especially true in response to natural and human disasters. In 2001, we joined together with churches across the city of Houston to bring relief from Tropical Storm Allison. We watched in horror that same year when the World Trade Center's twin towers in New York City fell on September 11, and sent encouragement and resources to friends there who were ministering in the aftermath.

We experienced an escalation in our role as relief responders with the tragic Indonesian ocean tsunami of 2004 and hurricanes Katrina and Rita in 2005. When the levees in New Orleans broke under the pressure of Katrina's battering, 80 percent of the city flooded and a mass evacuation began, with thousands of people headed our way. Imagine your city's population growing in a matter of two days by over 250,000 people—homeless, jobless, with no money or belongings except what they carried with them.

Imagine your city's population growing in a matter of two days by over 250,000 people—homeless, jobless, with no money or belongings except what they carried with them.

People began showing up at our office looking for help. For days, the entire first floor corridor of the office building we rent was a sea of desperately hurting humanity. Overwhelmed by what I saw that first day, I vowed that we would send no one away without helping them. The problem was, we had nothing to give them. But the body of Christ across the city and across the nation rose to the occasion.

At the time, our friend Kim Kossie-McKee worked for KSBJ radio. She called to tell us the station was directing their listeners to drop off gift cards at any YMCA, and the cards would be collected each afternoon. Would we be willing to receive and distribute the cards? I answered, "Yes!" without hesitating. By the end of that first day, every person who came through the office received at least one gift card to meet some immediate needs, along with prayer and hope.

We also had churches sending volunteers to help with phones, which were ringing nonstop. Truckloads of food and other necessities began to arrive from all around the country. Local businesses donated warehouse space or rented it for a minimal fee. One ministry donated cots that we gave to churches so they could set up shelters. A pastor friend came to offer manual labor. But when he saw our tiny staff working so hard to meet the astonishing amount of needs, he realized what we needed more than anything was prayer—so he mobilized a 24/7 prayer room in our fellowship hall.

During those first weeks of the crisis, we served 21,000 people in our office alone, while also helping to serve shelters and distribution centers at over a hundred locations throughout the city and at other locations in Texas, Louisiana, and Mississippi.

By God's providence, I had been serving as interim preacher at a church in Beaumont, Cathedral in the Pines. When Katrina hit, the elders agreed that the church could become a Somebody Cares Southeast Texas processing center for evacuees. Many evacuees were staying nearby at the Ford Arena, and I was asked to speak to bring a message of encouragement. Less than a week later—and only three weeks after Katrina—Hurricane Rita hit the area and these people and others who had evacuated had to evacuate once again, along with local residents. Because the church was already serving with us in Katrina relief, we were able to quickly set up as a distribution center for residents and other churches across the region, distributing food, materials, and housing teams. Because of relationships we had made during our work with the Kobe earthquake in Japan, we even had a team of Japanese relief workers join up with other teams and volunteers.

One of our partners estimates that Somebody Cares and all the ministries we networked with during that time facilitated over $40 million worth of goods and supplies, distributed through our Katrina and Rita relief partners throughout the Gulf.

> *How incredible are the possibilities available to us when we work together!*
> *Even the secular world will take notice.*

How incredible are the possibilities available to us when we work together! They are so incredible that even the secular world will take notice. The work of the faith-based community was even acknowledged by the federal government. H. James Towey, former director of the White House Office of Faith-Based and Community Initiatives, said the churches "are doing more than what they say they're doing—on nothing, because that's the passion of their heart."

PRINCIPLES THAT WORK

This is the principle of "mending the net." Jesus instructed the disciples to cast the net to bring in the harvest. (See Luke 5:4–6.) An individual or a church with only one fishing pole can catch only one fish at a time. But when we come together as a net that is mended and interlinked, even with our diversities and our distinctives, we become the *net that works.*

Richard Hinojosa, who was part of the original Somebody Cares Houston advisory board, was working as an associate pastor at Resurrection Life Church in Picayune, Mississippi, when Katrina hit. When his church began relief operations from their parking lot, Somebody Cares was one of the first organizations to direct trucks and food to their location.

"In the first two and a half weeks, over 23,000 cars came through the church parking lot and we were able to help 100,000 people," Richard said. "And that's a lot of people, especially when you're talking about a town that only has 15,000 residents! The community began to see that what the government couldn't do and what the agencies couldn't do, the church could do."

But most of all, Richard says, it was a time to truly comprehend the value of being connected. "You don't fully understand the importance of relationship until you are at a place where you really can't do something by yourself. After Katrina hit, we watched the body of Christ be the body of Christ. When the crisis hit, the network was already in place.

"For years, we heard Doug talk about 'mending the net.' It's not just a message now. We've lived it. It's real, and it works."

These principles are not just theory. They are proven principles that worked during the twenty years before the book *Somebody Cares* was published—when some of our biggest challenges were HIV, AIDS, gangs, at-risk youth, homelessness, and street kids—and they still work in every challenging situation we are facing today. We have not only seen them work in Houston, but adopted and multiplied in other locations around the U.S. and internationally through our Somebody Cares chapters, affiliates, church partners, and other relationships.

We have seen them work in the aftermath of hurricanes Ike, Harvey, Maria, Florence, Michael, and Laura; Superstorm Sandy in New York City; the earthquakes in Japan and Mexico City; Typhoon Haiyan in the Philippines; tornadoes in Moore, Oklahoma, and Birmingham, Alabama; and numerous other storms, wildfires, floods, and natural or human disasters.

We've seen these principles work in everyday challenges in communities, cities, and nations. And we have seen them work when shutdowns from a pandemic created social upheaval and caused economic hardship to families across our entire country.

As you read this book, we pray that your heart will be stirred with timeless testimonies from the early days of the ministry that began in the early 1980s, along with more recent updates throughout the book and in the closing chapter. And as we become that mended net, may we give ourselves to Jesus, so that He can cast us out together and bring in a great harvest of revival!

2

A TRUE WITNESS RESCUES LIVES

A true witness delivers souls,
but a deceitful witness speaks lies.
—Proverbs 14:25

You're all hypocrites!" the voice snarled. My radio host was taken aback, but I knew the caller's voice. He continued, "You bigots want to condemn everyone else to hell just because we don't do what you want."

"Mike," I said with a smile in my voice, "is that you?"

My astonished radio host looked at me with a question in his eyes that seemed to ask if he should flip the switch to cut off the caller. His call-in show drew Christian listeners, not the type he now heard. I looked at him across the microphones and smiled to allay his fears.

"What? Well…" the voice sputtered. This was unlike Mike, a man who had heckled at our meetings, harassed our street evangelists, and hurled legal and physical threats for over a year.

"Yeah, it's me," the voice said. "What are you going to do, get all your homophobe friends to pray for me?" His scornful laugh was weak.

"Let me ask you something, Mike." I shifted in my seat and put my face close to the microphone. "Your group hangs together, supports each other…all of you pretty much take each other's side, don't you?"

"Yeah!" he said, warming to the subject. "We're united, and we're gonna keep fighting until we shut you Christians up and expose you for the religious bigots you really are."

"So where were your friends when you needed help with your electric bill last month?"

"What? How do you know about my electric bill?"

"Because we paid it for you, Mike."

Astonished, Mike didn't know what else to say. Regardless of how he felt about us or what he had done to us, by coordinating with various groups in Houston, Christians were there when this AIDS patient needed help. And we continued to reach out to him.

I was on a ministry trip when I got a message saying Mike was in the hospital and wasn't doing well. Bill Small, who was part of our ministry and also battled HIV, went to visit him.

"Why did you take care of my bills?" Mike asked him. He still couldn't get it out of his head.

"The Lord put it on our hearts to do it because that's what Christians do," Bill replied. Then he prayed with Mike as he asked the Lord to come into his life. Mike cried as he received forgiveness for his sins. Within hours, he left this earth and found himself in the arms of a loving Savior.

THE BIRTH OF SOMEBODY CARES

The day I learned of Mike's salvation seemed like an eternity after my own conversion, yet it had been only ten years. I had been a fitness instructor back then, running my own exercise studio. I knew there was a God, yet I was living as if He didn't exist. Tired of my own hypocrisy and disgusted with my life, one night, I sat down in the back room of the studio, put my head in my hands, and prayed a simple prayer: "Lord, if You can use someone like me after all I have done to wound Your heart, I make myself available to You."

> *One night, I prayed a simple prayer: "Lord, if You can use someone like me after all I have done to wound Your heart, I make myself available to You."*

The year was 1981. God took me at my word. It seemed the Lord couldn't find enough needy people to send my way. I ran the exercise studio and then took a group to the streets most nights after the studio closed. There, we encountered runaways, strippers, and drug addicts, and brought them back to the studio, to the home of a widow who had offered to help, or to Greg's apartment, which a couple of us shared with him as roommates.

We couldn't meet every need, but we were willing to do what we could. Some new converts helped me transform the exercise studio into an outreach center. By 1983, we renamed it Turning Point Studio, a Christian Activities and Fellowship Center. The turning point in my life resulted in a turning point in the lives of others who needed Christ. Later, we became Turning Ministries International, which would become the parent ministry of Somebody Cares.

People's needs were far greater and more complex than what our tiny band of new converts could handle, so I began linking with other ministries in Houston. Together, we distributed the ordinary business card with which our ministry started. The card simply read: "Somebody Cares. Call 24 hours a day. 'A true witness rescues lives…' Prov. 14:25." A telephone number completed the message.

I will never forget one teenager who called the telephone number saying he needed immediate help to get off the streets while he had the courage to leave. The dilemma was that my apartment was crammed with people. I gave him the telephone numbers for other ministries. He called back later with desperation in his voice, saying none would take him. I put him on hold and went to the only vacant room in the apartment. Sitting on the lid of the closed toilet, I called out to God, asking Him what to do because I couldn't turn this young man away. The Lord spoke to my heart, saying, "There's always room for one more."

I went back to the telephone and promised that we'd find a place for him, even if it were the bathtub. A volunteer picked up the young man and brought him to the apartment. Just before they arrived, the telephone rang again, this time with a ministry that had just had a vacancy. They wanted to know if I had need for another bed.

Some situations were messier. One time, a bodyguard for a Dallas drug dealer called to say he was with a stripper and her Outlaw biker husband was out to kill him because he thought they were having an affair.

I went straight to the point. "Are you having an affair?"

"Well..." he stammered, before admitting it. I recommended some ministers in Dallas, but he insisted that he'd tried every one and they all said to call me. That puzzled me. I was young and halfway in the ministry, but still halfway in the business world. I had no money, no resources, and no way to help anyone with anything. All I had was availability.

Although it was a financial stretch, I bought two airline tickets for the bodyguard and the stripper. The widow who had volunteered her home housed one of them and I housed the other. Shortly thereafter, both committed their lives to Christ.

Then the stripper's husband tracked me down and called me, screaming at me in rage. I called him a wimp and said if he were a real man, he would submit himself to Christ and learn how to love his wife. Right there, during the telephone call, he started crying and said he was coming down to Houston, too. He came, got saved, stayed for quite a while to be discipled, got back together with his wife, and the two of them left. The bodyguard also eventually left and served on the staff of a Christian drug rehab center.

> *We had no money or official church support, yet we provided temporary housing for the homeless, conducted street witnessing and evangelistic crusades, and did Jericho marches around rock concerts.*

From such simple beginnings, the Somebody Cares message spread. We were a bunch of young people without money or official church support, yet we provided temporary housing for the homeless, conducted street witnessing and evangelistic crusades, did Jericho marches around rock concerts, and sponsored other activities geared to fellowship and discipleship. Drug addicts, alcoholics, strippers, and prostitutes—people considered too far gone by many—came to know Christ and moved on to good churches, jobs, businesses, and ministries.

All those years ago, when God grabbed hold of my heart, I knew if He could save me, He could save others. God established the heart of the ministry then and it has never changed, even though it has expanded to include not only meeting the needs of individuals, but has also allowed us to network and share the vision with other cities and nations about how believers can make a difference in their world.

Internationally, we are networking and linking with ministries, churches, schools, governments, and community leaders world-wide with the same message carried by the original little business card: "*A true witness rescues lives*" (or saves souls). We are not just an outreach of one group or denomination. Rather, we represent a united outreach of individual communities that includes feeding centers, crisis pregnancy intervention, gang prevention, men's and women's homes, drug abuse recovery, borderline teen intervention, foster care, job placement, and more. It is a joy to see what God has done in and through us as we join together to win our cities to Christ.

THE URGENCY OF THE HOUR

The message inherent in the words "Somebody Cares" is one that all people everywhere long to hear.

The message inherent in the words "Somebody Cares" is one that all people everywhere long to hear. For example, take a trip I made to Indonesia in 1998. Ministers there had requested that I speak at a large prayer conference. A dear friend, Paul Tan—who now serves on our board of directors—had started the Indonesian Relief Fund, on whose advisory board I served. I responded to the pastors' request with a request of my own. If I came to minister at their conference, I wanted them to set up feeding centers where Christians would provide food for the poor during the days I was there.

I made this request at a time of political turmoil. Militants were hunting and slaughtering Christians in some parts of the nation. Many Christians had lost their jobs and businesses, and many had fled the country. Headlines worldwide trumpeted the failed economy and national crisis in this fourth-largest nation on Earth, home to the world's largest Muslim population.

The Indonesian ministers said they had nothing to give, so I asked them just to do what Jesus did when He faced a hungry multitude and had only a child's lunch with which to feed them: take what you have, bless it, and start giving it away. They agreed to try.

A team from Houston—comprised of Hispanics, Asians, pastors, and intercessors— accompanied me to Indonesia. Once there, we saw what the impoverished Christians had accomplished. Pastor Jimmy and his group had set up thirty-five feeding centers called Free Lunch from the Lord, Somebody Cares.

As a result of the Christians' efforts to feed the poor, one hundred pastors were asked to meet with then President B. J. Habibi, and they invited me to come to the meeting. I hated to change my airline ticket because I didn't have the money for the additional expense, but the ministers urged me, saying this was unprecedented in their nation's history. I agreed to join them. During the meeting, President Habibi, on national television, praised the efforts and compassion of these Christians and officially endorsed what became known as the Somebody Cares Indonesia Movement.

After ministering at their conference, they took our team to outlying areas so we could minister to the rural poor. We drove in vans from location to location. Pastors grimaced as they saw settlements of hundreds of people living in garbage dumps and hundreds more under bridges. A few of the pastors had never traveled outside their area to see the plight of their people. At one stop in a mountain village, a local pastor introduced us to a young man.

> *Pastors grimaced as they saw settlements of hundreds of people living in garbage dumps and hundreds more under bridges.*

"He has won his entire village to Christ," the pastor announced through interpreters.

"Then I need to wash his feet," I said, "because I have not yet won mine."

Some of the pastors seemed dismayed at my request, but they found a bowl of water and some rags. I was sincere in honoring this young man for winning his city.

Afterward, the pastors loaded back into the vans and traveled to the next stop in silence as the impact of what they had just witnessed settled over them. When I asked about their silence, they said they were speechless because an American minister had washed the feet of one of their poorest countrymen. When we returned to Jakarta, one pastor told the others, "This man didn't honor us for holding a nationwide event, but he honored the man who had led every person he knew to Christ. He has shown us what truly matters."

Traveling on to Malaysia, the movement we left behind spread and gained momentum. I received a call at my hotel room and learned that the governor of Java now wanted to meet with me and help us bring to his area the Somebody Cares Indonesia feeding centers, as they were now being called. Again, I changed my airline tickets and went back to accompany local pastors to the governor's mansion. God gave me a prophetic message for this Muslim leader: if he blessed God's people, God would bless him. He bowed his head and said he wanted to be a friend. He, too, went on television to endorse the Somebody Cares movement.

During the eight months after we left, Indonesian Christians managed to feed three million people. The pastors were overjoyed that as the Christians gave, God multiplied their efforts until sites in several cities provided "Lunch from the Lord," based on what Jesus had done with the hungry multitude. They followed the Somebody Cares model and involved hundreds of churches and ministries to accomplish their agenda. When they came together in unity, even a seemingly hostile government had to acknowledge them.

Years later, after the tragic tsunami of 2004 wiped out entire communities of Indonesia, Somebody Cares was able to bypass governmental red tape and supply aid quickly to the areas of devastation because we had already laid this foundation. Working alongside our Indonesian friends, we were able to be among the first responders on the ground bringing relief.

With all the crises in our world today—from escalating racial tensions to pandemics to polarizing political issues—it is impossible to ignore the intensity and urgency of the hour.

With just a glance at all the crises in our world today—from escalating racial tensions to pandemics to polarizing political issues—it is impossible to ignore the intensity and urgency of the hour. Simply by being born to this generation, you and I have been called *for such a time as this,* to reach out to people—from paupers to presidents.

The Creator of the universe intends for your life and mine to shape the destiny of this world. When I met Christ, something changed inside me so that I no longer lived just for myself. My life was not my own. The day any of us comes to Christ, our lives have new meaning and purpose. Our Father has a job for us to accomplish.

Jesus revealed Himself that we might have a relationship with Him, but that's not all. As an outcome of that relationship, we are called to be ministers of reconciliation and witnesses who rescue lives. (See Acts 26:16; Proverbs 14:25.) We can impact this generation with the gospel of Christ, which *is the power of God to salvation for everyone who believes* (Romans 1:16).

We have a window of time to reach the multitudes still in the valley of decision. The question is, *Will we answer the call?* To say yes, we must understand the awesome responsibility God has entrusted to us, His church.

MINISTERS OF RECONCILIATION

In 1983, I was driving with a sixteen-year-old street kid who hadn't eaten in four days and was looking for a ministry that could care for him. On the way back to Houston on Highway 59, I saw a hitchhiker with a sign that read, "Australian." As I passed the hitchhiker, God spoke to my heart to stop, so I pulled over, backed up, and picked him up. That one act unwittingly started him on the ride of his life.

"G'day mate," Andrew Merry said as he jumped into the car. He asked if I would drive him to a youth hostel to stay for a night. He explained that he was traveling casually on a one-year trip to see the world. I told him he could ride with us to my exercise studio and I'd try to find a place for him to stay. I left Andrew and the street kid to sleep in one room while I went to my office to make some calls. After a while, Andrew came in, asking about the street kid. The teenager had run off with Andrew's backpack, which held his passport and money, among other things. As a result, Andrew was stuck in Houston much longer than he had planned.

Before landing in Houston, Andrew had met a young New Zealand woman named Lynette, who was also traveling around the world on a one-year pass. Lynette had just become a Christian before leaving for overseas and realized she would be better off without a non-Christian boyfriend. She resisted Andrew's romantic interest and they remained friends.

On Andrew's second or third night in Houston, I took him to a Christian concert at Astroworld. He was amazed at what Christianity actually meant. Within a few days, he gave his heart to Christ and decided to stay with us for six weeks to become discipled and grounded in his new faith. I have never seen a young convert soak in the gospel as quickly and earnestly as Andrew Merry did.

He regaled us with stories of his life Down Under. Andrew was a triathlete and a coach who had tried hard to party his life away. While driving drunk just before leaving the country, he heard something say, "Slow down." He immediately slowed his car. Rounding the next corner, he saw a person who had fallen in the street and whom he would have run over had he not slowed down. Clearly, God was directing Andrew's steps.

Finally, the day came for us to bid Andrew farewell so he could continue on to Europe, via New York, where he met up with Lynette again. Naturally, he couldn't wait to tell Lynette he was now a Christian, but she ignored him, believing he was just trying to impress her. Andrew's new habit of witnessing to others eventually won her over. While in Europe, their friendship began to blossom. By the time they returned to their own countries, Andrew had changed so much that his testimony was written up in the local newspapers. Andrew and Lynette continued their correspondence and later became engaged. For many years, the Merrys pastored a thriving church, Ocean Grove Baptist Fellowship, now known as The Wave, before leaving to serve for several years in leadership with Compassion Australia.

On the road to Damascus, Jesus told Saul, *"I have appeared to you for this purpose, to make you a minister and a witness"* (Acts 26:16). Jesus revealed Himself first for the sake of saving Saul, but also so that Saul would fulfill a God-ordained purpose. This is what Andrew also learned.

> *The first revelation any of us receives from God is the revelation of the work of the cross and the power of His resurrection.*

The first revelation any of us receives from God is the revelation of the work of the cross—that we have been bought with Christ's own blood shed on Calvary—and the power of His resurrection. This is the revelation of Jesus, our Savior and our Redeemer, that leads us to salvation. In that redemption, we are given a greater purpose.

When he received his commission from the Lord, Saul became an apostle of the good news. God changed his name to Paul to sever ties with his old identity and old life. Paul now burned with a holy passion to make Christ known. He was a catalyst for whole villages and cities coming to Christ. He wrote:

> *Much more then, having now been justified by His blood, we shall be saved from wrath through Him. For if when we were enemies we were reconciled to God through the death of His Son, much more, having been reconciled, we shall be saved by His life. And not only that, but we also rejoice in God through our Lord Jesus Christ, through whom **we have now received the reconciliation**.* (Romans 5:9–11)

Through the blood of God's Son, we are reconciled to Him and made joint heirs with Christ. We give *"thanks to the Father who has qualified us to be partakers of the inheritance of the saints in the light"* (Colossians 1:12). Once we were separated from the Father by our sin, but now we are redeemed and restored to a right relationship with Him. No greater peace or joy exists than to know we belong to Christ. But this is just the beginning of our journey as believers.

> *Therefore, if anyone is in Christ, he is a new creation; old things have passed away; behold, all things have become new. Now all things are of God, who has reconciled us to Himself through Jesus Christ, and has given us **the ministry of reconciliation**, that is, that God was in Christ reconciling the world to Himself, not imputing their trespasses to them, and has committed to us the word of reconciliation. Now then, we are ambassadors for Christ, as though God were pleading through us: we implore you on Christ's behalf, be reconciled to God. For He made Him who knew no sin to be sin for us, that we might become the righteousness of God in Him.*
>
> (2 Corinthians 5:17–21)

As soon as we are reconciled to Christ, we become *ministers* of reconciliation. That is our calling. Regardless of the specific way in which we serve God's kingdom, our primary purpose is to minister to others.

As we live purposefully before the Lord, our lives exude the Lord's presence, and others are drawn to Him through us to find their place of reconciliation with the living God. People all around us are searching and longing for the hope they see living inside of you and me. How will they know this hope unless we are faithful to be His witnesses?

*People all around us are searching and longing
for the hope they see living inside us.
How will they know this hope unless we are faithful
to be His witnesses?*

Before Andrew Merry exercised his gifts or talents, he first became a minister of reconciliation right where he was to those around him. Hundreds have now come to Christ through his ministry of reconciliation, which is his first and basic purpose.

PASSION FOR GOD AND THE LOST

A passion for God compels us to share the good news with the lost. Yet how many of us have questioned if God can truly use us to reach the lost? Many believers wonder what they have to offer, not realizing the power of God's Spirit abiding in them. The same power that resurrected Christ from the dead dwells in our mortal bodies. (See Romans 8:11.) God does not entrust us with this power so that we can glory in it. His power dwells in us so His love can flow through us, drawing others to Him.

We are never too insignificant, too unnoticed, or too weak to exercise God's power. Some people point to a Scripture about judgments of the last days, with earthquakes and famines. (See Luke 21:11.) Even though God says a shaking is coming (see Hebrews 12:26), one sentence pops out: *"But it will turn out for you as an occasion for testimony"* (Luke 21:13). Bad news, weakness, and difficulty are opportunities for the Christian.

No matter what you and I may go through, regardless of the circumstances of our lives or the setbacks we face, we have the opportunity to be a witness to others. Whatever the trials, we will overcome by the blood of the Lamb and the word of our testimony. (See Revelation 12:11.) We will see all things work together for the good of those who love God and are called according to His purpose. (See Romans 8:28.) No matter the intensity, there will be an opportunity for our witness and our testimony. Will we recognize the opportunity?

Almost two years after Mike, the radio caller, died from AIDS, I was ministering at a local church in another city in Texas, where I told Mike's story. After the meeting, a woman came to me, crying. The harder she tried to speak, the more she seemed to cry.

"That," she finally said, "was my son."

For years, she had prayed for Mike, even though their relationship was strained because of his lifestyle and activism against everything that had to do with God. Yet while he lived, she had prayed. She did her part. Others did their parts. As a result, today Mike is in heaven with our Lord.

We live in awesome times. Let's not miss our opportunities. The job at hand is larger than any one person, church, or ministry can handle. We can only reach our communities if we all work together. It starts by each of us individually asking the Lord how we are to exercise our ministry of reconciliation and how we are to link up with others in the body of Christ.

3

SOMETHING BIGGER
THAN OURSELVES

*But rise and stand on your feet; for I have appeared to you
for this purpose, to make you a minister and a witness both
of the things which you have seen and of the things which I
will yet reveal to you.*
—Acts 26:16

One night in the early '80s, a young couple stood on a street
corner in the Montrose area of Houston, which at that time had
one of the highest crime rates in Texas. Montrose, also called

Lower Westheimer, was a haven for runaways and filled with prostitutes, pimps, drug dealers, and flamboyant cross-dressers. Making it even worse, youth and yuppies from suburbia found their entertainment cruising Lower Westheimer on weekend nights. Their presence and economic support helped to establish a sad and perverse lifestyle.

The young couple on the corner looked typical for that neighborhood—young teenagers who had no means of support other than to sell themselves on the streets. It was apparent they had lived on the streets for a while, even though their youthfulness had not yet given way to hardness. Lori was cute, with delicate features and a soft voice. In any home in America, her mother would have scolded her for wearing too much makeup. She was attractive enough without it. Brandon was thin, still not filled out, with sad eyes and dirty-blond hair. He smelled of cigarettes and sweat.

What captured my heart was the stroller between them. Children with children of their own. The stroller, holding a precious newborn and a toddler, was parked right in front of a pay phone where Lori and Brandon took their calls. They would wait for the phone to ring, then Brandon would watch the children while Lori waded through the bumper-to-bumper traffic to find the caller and turn a trick. If the call was for Brandon, Lori would babysit while Brandon serviced the caller.

Such a sight still overwhelms me. When I see it, I want to run up and yell, "Stop! You don't have to live like this. Quick, come with me!" That's about what I did with Brandon and Lori. I told them the good news of the gospel and shared with them my care and concern, convincing them to come home with me.

At one point, there were seventeen people living in an apartment with me. I trusted the Lord to provide food for them each day.

After I had been in this ministry for a while, E. Z. Jones, who led a local men's ministry, paid for me to have my own apartment. At one point, seventeen people lived in it with me. I didn't have the funds to feed anyone, but I took Brandon, Lori, and their children home anyway, believing that a night in my home, even without food, would be better than a night on the streets.

One day, E. Z. came to the apartment and saw all the people. He gave me one of those blank, disbelieving looks and said, "Doug, how are you feeding all these people?"

I smiled and told him we trusted the Lord to provide each day. We had witnessed true miracles of God's provision as we prayed and stayed focused on our calling. People would leave groceries at the door or provide for our needs in other ways. God does not ask the same of every person, but He does ask each of us to do what we can. We proved that even a home-cooked meal could be a part of fulfilling God's call.

E. Z.'s heart was touched by what he saw. He and his wife Lena started providing food for inner-city ministries by establishing a Christian businessmen's network known as Luv Ya Houston. E. Z. recognized what we were learning—that each of us has a vital role in reaching people within our communities.

Through those early experiences in reaching out to people like Brandon and Lori, I saw a glimpse of what God intended for every believer. The job was far bigger than anyone could handle alone. The number of homeless people, drug addicts, and troubled teens is enormous. Other lost people cover their true needs with masks of success and affluence. Whatever the situation, every person is hungry for truth and love. And all believers are called to become *part of something bigger than themselves* to extend that love.

When all believers in the body of Christ work together, we can meet people's physical needs. People who encounter our true care and concern for them are drawn to the love of Christ operating in us. Each individual, church, or ministry, working together and doing their part, can impact a whole city with the gospel.

> *Whatever the situation, every person is hungry for truth and love. And all believers are called to become part of something bigger than themselves to extend that love.*

In the case of Lori and Brandon, the call of the streets was stronger than their ability to resist. Time and again, they returned to their dangerous lifestyle. They eventually contracted diseases and lost their children to state government. Their young, promising lives came to an end without ever fulfilling their potential. But they knew who Jesus is.

We may work with an individual off and on for many years before the breakthrough comes in his or her life. Sometimes, we never see it. Yet no labor for the Lord is in vain. God is faithful to watch over every seed sown into a soul.

WE ARE THE ONLY PLAN GOD HAS

Bill Anderson, who pastored Calvary Baptist Church and was also part of Somebody Cares Tampa Bay, shared this story from his childhood at one of their meetings in 1997:

God stabbed my heart about unity long before I was saved. My father was killed in an oil field accident when I was just five weeks old. My dear mother, who lives in Clearwater, Florida, now is ninety-eight years old and loves God with all her heart. One day as young teenagers, my sister and I were fighting. My mother came to me and it was one of the rare times that I saw fear in her eyes. She is a very strong woman. She had to be, for more than sixty years now, she has been without a man by her side. Raising four children by herself, she made it one day at a time, as she says, "by the grace of God." Mother sat my sister and me down and wept as she said, "You *have* to get along because you're all I have." That stabbed me.

Listen, there are not two brides. There's only one bride. We are the only bride Christ has. If we don't do it right, nobody can.

God has no other plan. We are it. That means He has confidence that Christ in us can meet the challenge. Our common purpose is to see lost souls come to the Lord. Jesus showed us that a grain of seed must die for there to be fruitfulness. (See John 12:24.) This is true in our lives individually, as we die to our own agendas, and it is true for the body of Christ.

We are called to sow the seed of our lives into the soil of souls. This doesn't mean we come together in unity only for citywide Christian gatherings, but that we desire to see lives changed— people turned from darkness to light. (See Acts 26:18.) We're not looking for unity for unity's sake, because unity never works without a purpose. And that's the point of Acts 26. Unity is not the goal; it is the by-product.

To have genuine unity, we have to have a purpose far greater than ourselves. Let us not look for unity as the lowest common denominator, which always leads to compromise. Let us look for unity with the highest common denominator—a great purpose found in passion for God and compassion for souls.

We are called to reach the unchurched with the good news, which we've traditionally called revival. If what we do doesn't equate into changed lives and lost souls coming to Christ, it falls short of being a true revival.

> *If what we do doesn't equate into changed lives and lost souls coming to Christ, it falls short of being a true revival.*

THEY SAID IT WOULDN'T LAST

From our beginnings in the early 1980s, we made ongoing efforts to network ministries and churches. By the mid-1980s, we were serving alongside other ministries on a regular basis. Relationships blossomed and strengthened as we all worked together in weekly street evangelism. Unknown soldiers of the gospel reached out to prostitutes, drug addicts, and street kids for years. They are true heroes of God's kingdom.

Starting in 1986, and for ten years afterward, we sponsored an annual evangelism conference to link inner-city ministries with mainline suburban churches. We provided a place to share strategies and establish a system of referral to help those in need.

People told me that a conference focusing on unifying the body of Christ toward a common goal seemed far-fetched and wouldn't work. Critics said churches and other ministries would not work together because they wanted to do their own thing. So I prayed about it and got together with other local ministers. We decided that regardless of who might not cooperate, many would, and it was time to combine forces! We set these goals:

- ✦ **Synergy.** We recognized that unifying various ministries would enlarge and augment the efforts of each ministry working on its own and promote fruitfulness.

- ✦ **Referrals.** We committed to establishing a referral list of proven ministries.

- ✦ **Guidance.** We endeavored to give guidance to people who wanted to serve God but didn't know how.

✦ **Honoring the local church.** We encouraged people to support, encourage, and work in their local churches.

The bottom line was and is to serve the people who need ministry. Too many times, we didn't know what to do with people who had AIDS, runaways, or church members whose children were involved in gangs. Certainly, every church and ministry couldn't operate its own hospice, feeding center, or home for unwed mothers. But linked together, these same churches and ministries were able to say, "Wait a minute, I know who can help you!"

The annual conference allowed us to recognize ministries already functioning in our city and, in some cases, it birthed new ministries. As we combined the outreach efforts into one place, we discovered areas of need the church had not yet addressed. For example, God touched people's hearts to work with the Houston police department when we realized there were no Christians active in dealing with the gang problem.

At one conference, John Hazzard brought the audience to tears. He was the least likely person anyone would have expected to get saved. A drug mule for nationally organized gangs, he was AIDS-infected from sharing needles while shooting heroin, a habit acquired at age fourteen. Members of our ministry team worked with John when he became serious about God, and he became a changed man.

John had been in several drug rehabilitation centers and mental hospitals and only had a third-grade education. We found a tutor to help him learn to read and write, so he could study the Bible for himself. His first volunteer project at our office was to put our Rolodex in alphabetical order.

When John was told he had only six months to live, a tutor might have seemed an extravagance, but John lived for another four years and became an integral part of the ministry.

We made a multipurpose room filled with boxes and equipment available to John and anyone else who wandered in. In it, we placed a donated television, VCR, and stacks of Christian teaching tapes like those found in the homes of many Christians. Those tapes discipled John while we were busy. One-on-one discipleship occurred in the evenings. Soon John began volunteering to help with mailings and then to reach out to others.

Through John and his ministry, God opened doors for the salvation of many others who needed freedom from various bondages and addictions. Five prayer and discipleship groups sprang up. Close friendships developed between John and several people, including Gabi Soltau, a missionary from Germany who moved to Houston and joined our staff. Gabi now serves as pastor of prayer and intercession at Houston's Encourager Church, and she travels abroad, reproducing the DNA of this ministry as she teaches on prayer.

When I took John with me to Houston Baptist University to help teach a friend's class, the distinguished Bible instructor came to John afterward, shook his hand, and said he'd never heard anyone lay out Scripture as John had.

As John's body deteriorated from AIDS, his light shone brighter and brighter. He opened his home to some and continued to witness with us. He went on fourteen missionary trips, even as his body wasted away.

John's T-cell count was only twenty-three and he weighed just eighty pounds when he asked one of our ministers to take him to buy five new shirts, which he washed and ironed himself to attend what would be his last conference. At the conference, he encouraged each of us to do what God says, to set aside differences and combine our efforts to reach others like him who only needed an opportunity to hear the truth. He battled for every breath, and each word gripped our hearts.

At that conference, John shared one of his favorite quotes by Andrew Murray (1828–1917), a preacher in Scotland and South Africa: "Give up on no man as long as he is alive; until he is laid in the grave, give up on no man." After John said this, he looked at a few of us and said, "I thank God that Doug and George and all of my Turning Point family did not give up on me."

SOUNDING A TRUMPET

At each of these annual conferences, we focused on a specific theme, such as "revival equates into changed lives" or "evangelism is an outcome of relationship," always stressing that we must *become part of something bigger than ourselves.* Workshops equipped Christian workers. Ministers and laypersons alike challenged participants to submit to their local churches, to work with other ministers, to exercise spiritual warfare, to stand in the gap for souls, and to look beyond their immediate communities to impact the entire city.

The mission statement for Turning Point, the ministry that birthed Somebody Cares, was: "Preparing a people for the coming of the Lord through a message of *consecration, commitment,* and *action.*" For years, we have challenged those in our ministry to personally commit to the motto, "A Call to Consecration, Commitment, and Action." Many who came through our ministry in the early days tell us how this is something has stuck with them and impacted their decision to this day.

The Lord is calling for a united church, which requires a message of:

+ **Consecration:** being separated unto God, recognizing His holiness, our own unrighteousness, and His grace

+ **Commitment:** not just "romancing" God and His work but acknowledging our responsibility to obey Him and letting that knowledge provoke us to action

+ **Action:** turning our responsibility into concrete obedience

From our individual relationships with the Lord, we commit to availability for His service. We must move beyond declarations and proclamations into action and become a tangible expression of Christ. Then we unite as the body of Christ and take action to reach out with the gospel. When we do these things, the Lord *will* transform our communities.

But it takes prayer, diligence, and consistency to see breakthroughs. We see communities change as the church agrees to work together for the common purpose of reaching the lost and the unchurched.

> *The synergy created when ministries work together exponentially increases our potential to impact lives.*

The synergy created when ministries work together exponentially increases our potential to impact lives. One group may have a gift to work with unwed mothers, while another group provides legal services for them. Another ministry will work with those who are HIV-positive, while a partner church provides food and clothing. If a homeless shelter is in disrepair, a ministry provides the volunteers to renovate it.

There is hope for our generation, and we are called to share that hope. But seeing God's kingdom built requires sacrifice and dying to our own rights and agendas. To fulfill our purpose of leading a generation to Christ, not only must we be reconciled to God, but we must also be reconciled to one another. The world is looking for answers. God will draw them to us for those answers as they see our love for Him and for each other.

Revival will not come unless we are willing to get past the things that have hindered our relationship with the Lord and with our brothers and sisters in Christ. If we want true revival, we must be willing to work with brothers and sisters of a different denomination or nationality. We must be willing to get past differences within the body of Christ. And most important, we must be in right relationship with God and with those in the church.

Eventually, more than two hundred ministries and churches agreed to work together to impact the greater Houston area. Turning Point Ministries was the umbrella organization that allied them into a network known as Somebody Cares. Many ministers signed a covenant of unity, stating that because they agreed on the basic tenets of their faith, they would work together, serve one another, and keep the unity of their faith and fellowship. I also call it the "no competition" clause.

These ministers were not just *talking* about the problems in their city; they were *working* in practical ways to impact the city at a grassroots level. Unity with a purpose is an action and a commitment to see a great harvest, not only in a particular city, but also across this nation and in all the nations of the world.

> Unity with a purpose is an action and a commitment to see a great harvest, not only in a particular city, but in all the nations of the world.

Somebody Cares does not actually create new works; we merely identify what God is already doing. Ministers and their congregants, who are already touching lives, are linking arms with others who are doing the same. We recognize that we are not the only network; we simply desire to identify and link together those who are already reaching out at a grassroots level.

The heart of Somebody Cares can be summed up in the slight change of words we made to that business card from decades ago: *"Somebody Cares. Because of what Jesus Christ has done for us, area churches and ministries want you to know that we care."* This is a message that communicates to the unchurched that God cares for them, and He cares for them through you and me.

JOY IN THE HARVEST

What joy we experience when even one person responds to the gospel! It may take years to see the fruit of our labors, and after countless hours of witnessing and counseling, there is often heartbreak when the truth is rejected. Yet each person who receives and accepts help is one more soul snatched from the devil's clutches.

Years after the day I brought Brandon and Lori into my apartment—a ministry attempt that could be viewed as a dismal failure—I met a couple, Dick and Debbie, whose mission was to adopt and rehabilitate discarded children. They heard me talk about *throwaway children* at one of our conferences, and the term captured their hearts. A week later, they were asked to provide foster care for a child from Casa de Esperanza, a Catholic-run orphanage. Then they received the child's sibling, and eventually adopted both children.

Through a coincidence that can only have come through the faithfulness of God, their two adopted children are Brandon and Lori's precious little ones who were raised on the streets while their parents prostituted themselves. Our heavenly Father was looking out for those precious babies all along. God is a Father to the fatherless. (See Psalm 68:5.)

Dick and Debbie adopted a total of seven children. When combined with the ten children in their blended family, they have a grand total of seventeen children.

The children they adopted were considered high risk. Two of them came from a home where they had to fight the family pets for food. The parents thought it was amusing to set the food on the floor and watch their children fight the dog and cat for the right to eat. One of their children—who now enjoys a home, family, siblings, food, and clothing—was interviewed early in the adoption process. She had come from living in a field, then was found abandoned in a boxcar.

The interviewers asked her, "Did you have a tent in that field?"

"No," she responded, "but sometimes we had newspapers."

One child couldn't sleep at night, so one of Dick and Debbie's grown children used to crawl into the bed to sleep with her. Another was so afraid of men she couldn't allow herself to get near Dick. Later, she proudly showed me photos of her "first date." It was with Dick, her daddy, who had brought flowers for her and taken her out to dinner. Simple for some, yet a milestone for this girl.

Government agencies observed the love and care that children received in Dick and Debbie's home. They noticed the remarkable changes in the lives of these young people who came from backgrounds that were so abusive it was feared they would be marked for life. Instead, they are marked for a life more abundant through Jesus! They are working through their issues, not running from them or covering them up. They are finding healing and freedom, and no one would guess what they've been through. The love of Jesus has brought wholeness to their lives.

Dick and Debbie mastered the governmental red tape that scares most people away from adoption and became part of a team from Somebody Cares Houston that developed Hope in Houston, a citywide church awareness campaign with a goal to see Houston's orphans adopted by linking government and private agencies with the body of Christ to place these children. Debbie has since gone to be with the Lord, but she left a beautiful legacy through her family.

YWAM Houston, which works with street kids in the same Montrose area where our ministry outreaches started, also served with our Hope in Houston campaign. They later added initiatives to their own ministry that targeted children of street kids, including a Mom's Day Out, foster care training, and an adoption agency.

WHAT ABOUT YOUR CITY?

What has taken place and is continuing to take place in Houston can happen anywhere. What about your city? Do you have a strategy to work with other believers to reach your city? There's no better time to get started than now.

> *Do you have a strategy to work with other believers to reach your city? There's no better time to get started than now.*

I thank God for the various ministries that have reached out in Houston and laid a foundation for those who are serving today. The Spanish-language Somebody Cares, called *Alguien Se Interesa*, reached our Hispanic community, which in the 1990s accounted for 30 percent of Houston's 4.5 million people. Due to the collaborative efforts of many Hispanic churches and ministries, we were able to distribute the Alguien Se Interesa Bible across the city. Today, we continue our outreach through Magda Hermida Ministries and many other Hispanic and Latino churches.

His Touch Ministries cared for those who were HIV-positive. I am reminded of the HIV-positive people who came through Turning Point—John, Isaiah, Johnny, Bill, Mark, and others who have now gone home to be with Jesus because of this terrible disease. Our ministry team understands the sleepless nights, the round-the-clock care, and the grief of family members.

Victory Inner-City Ministries worked with former drug addicts and gang members. I remember Robert, a former gang member who got out of the gang, avoided attempted hits on his life, and yet died of cancer. Months before his death, Robert gave his life to Christ. I spoke with him just days before his death and asked if there was anything we could do for him. His only concern was for his wife and child. He is remembered as a loving husband and father because he became a new man in Christ.

I also remember ministering at a memorial service for a teen killed in a drive-by gang shooting. He was a junior high school student killed for his designer athletic shoes.

These stories are about real people who left family members behind. That is why the work of each ministry is so vital. My heart is stirred to stand in the gap for frontline workers and the people they reach. These people need encouragement to press on each day and *"not grow weary while doing good"* (Galatians 6:9).

There are so many still to be reached! Together, with each of us doing our part, we can make a difference. If we walk in a right relationship with the Lord and with each other, His light will shine through us and draw people to Him.

How will our communities be reached? By our *intercession* and then our *intervention* for the multitudes hanging in the balance of eternity.

4

A KINGDOM BUILT
ON RELATIONSHIP

*We were well pleased to impart to you not only the gospel of
God, but also our own lives, because you had become dear to us.*
—1 Thessalonians 2:8

Etched into my heart are the names and faces of the people we
reached on the streets in those early years. Some did not make it
out of street life. Some did but died young due to the consequences
of their choices. There are, however, many success stories of young

men and women who left street life behind. Not only were they discipled, but they also became active in discipling others. There is no greater joy than seeing a wayward life radically turned around by God.

As we worked on the streets and as the network of ministries we worked with began to grow, we realized that the kingdom of God is built on relationship. As friendships formed between young ministers and laypersons who had the same heartbeat to reach hurting people, God began to link us together to address the diverse situations we encountered.

> *Not everyone is called to street ministry or to the inner cities, but each of us is called to fulfill the work of an evangelist.*

Not everyone is called to street ministry or to the inner cities, but each of us is called to fulfill the work of an evangelist. (See 2 Timothy 4:5.) Not everyone has a special gift as an evangelist, but we can all be living witnesses. (See Acts 1:8; Ephesians 4:11.) Each day, our lives can testify of Christ's love, and we can do our part as we develop our relationship with the Lord and He gives us His heart for people.

HAND IN HAND TO REACH THE LOST

Mohawk frequented the Lower Westheimer area of Houston where the street kids hung out. Covered with tattoos and filled with hatred, the only people he got along with were skinheads. As a person of Asian descent, I was the unlikeliest person this skinhead would listen to, let alone trust.

Still, when I saw Mohawk sitting on a curb, I would sit down to talk with him. Soon he actually wanted to spend time with me. We started working out at a gym together. Eventually, I could tell that his initial hatred toward me was gone. Mohawk was building a respect toward the people of God, which translated into a respect toward the things of God. Love was beginning to break through.

As teams of ministers worked with Mohawk and others like him, this young man and the other street kids saw love in action. A local Baptist minister named Curt Williams had come to the streets independently and joined me on many nights to talk with young people. We established a place called The Refuge at 408 Westheimer, right in the middle of the kids' hangout area. Volunteers staffed it. The young people knew that when they wanted help, regardless of the time of day or night, someone would be there for them.

When the *Houston Chronicle* ran a story about street evangelism and the change it was bringing to the city's young people, Curt and I told the reporters that our mission was not just to get troubled teens off the streets but also to get them into environments where they could quit running from their problems. When the kids said they wanted help, we either provided them housing or referred them to someone who could put them up.

Based on Curt's heart's desire to disciple young men once they left street life, he and his wife Shelley founded Youth-Reach Houston, a licensed foster home for teenage boys. I am honored to serve on Youth-Reach's board of advisors. Since 1984, Youth-Reach has been an outstanding ministry for discipling young people in our city. They now are working in Alabama as well.

BEYOND SURVIVAL TO DISCIPLESHIP

Every street kid I've ever met has the need to be loved and to belong to a family. In their street culture vernacular, they often say, "If one of us is in trouble, we cut for each other," meaning they stand up for each other. They're saying they're one family, one culture, and have one purpose: survival. But this is true only to a point. In the game of survival, each person ultimately ends up looking out for himself.

> *Every street kid I've ever met has the need to be loved and to belong to a family.*
> *But in the game of survival, each person ultimately ends up looking out for himself.*

Over time, Mohawk realized there was more to life than just survival on the streets. He eventually succumbed to regular, healthy doses of love and left street life and his street name behind. He ended up helping other young people at Youth-Reach Houston as a Christian counselor named Dave. We praise God for the dramatic changes in his life. At the same time, we recognize that many more like him still need to be reached.

At times, the Lord may speak to our hearts about an entire people group for whom we are to pray and reach out to with the gospel message. But how do we minister to different nationalities and cultures? What will it take to understand them and meet their needs? Understanding begins with gaining an appreciation for those in the body of Christ who come from different backgrounds. As we learn to love and care for each other, we will likewise be able to minister to unbelievers in various people groups.

The body of Christ's ability to embrace different groups must begin with each believer's own desire. As each of us gets to know Christian brothers and sisters of different cultural groups and we come to understand the issues they face, we will see how much we need one another in order to make a difference in people's lives. We may not be able to reach a particular community others have been called to serve, but we can support their efforts and build each other up.

Understanding begins with gaining an appreciation for those in the body of Christ who come from different backgrounds.

PREPARING THE BRIDE

God is preparing a bride for His Son. Part of that preparation is the necessity of getting past obstacles that hinder our relationships within the body of Christ.

The church that God is preparing is radiant with His character and full of charity, with no division in her heart. She does not quarrel over rights or set boundaries for her service. She willingly offers herself for the sake of the Bridegroom.

The prophet Micah wrote about the people of God who will gather at His holy mountain to form a strong nation. (See Micah 4:1–7.) This is a theme that challenges us to lay down our weapons of warfare and exchange them with harvesting tools.

He shall judge between many peoples, and rebuke strong nations afar off; they shall beat their swords into plowshares, and their spears into pruning hooks; nation shall not lift up sword against nation, neither shall they learn war anymore.

(Micah 4:3)

As we gather together with a passion for God and with compassion for those who do not yet know the Lord, we can become the bride described in biblical prophecy. This kind of unity will only occur as we focus on the harvest, which is God's primary calling to the church today. In the world, we will continue to hear of warring factions, but there is a group of people who are setting aside their differences, adopting a common identity and a common purpose to overcome a common enemy.

Micah goes on to speak of the kind of people who will make up the harvest:

"In that day," says the Lord, *"I will assemble the lame, I will gather the outcast and those whom I have afflicted; I will make the lame a remnant, and the outcast a strong nation."*

(Micah 4:6–7)

What a beautiful sight that will be! Already the Lord is beginning to gather His people in such a way, taking outcasts and making us into *"a strong nation."* It is not unlike the weaving of multicolored threads into a finished fabric.

A COAT OF MANY COLORS

In Genesis 37, we read about a beautifully woven coat presented to Joseph by his father Jacob. Imagine for a moment the beauty of the tunic that Jacob gave to Joseph. That coat must have been brilliant in color and quality. As its colors were interwoven, a beautiful fabric emerged.

When I think of the coat of many colors, I see a picture of the bride God desires to present to Jesus Christ. As the body of Christ becomes a united bride, we become a coat woven together of many colors. Though we are diverse in ethnicity and culture, through Christ, we are knit together from every background to become a strong nation. We are now part of the culture of Christ.

Something happened after Joseph received the coat; his brothers resented him for the favor he received from his father and for the dream he shared with them. In their jealousy, they sought to destroy Joseph.

We must guard against animosity, jealousy, envy, or bitterness that would divide us from other brothers and sisters.

A similar scenario can happen within the body of Christ. We must guard against animosity, jealousy, envy, or bitterness that would divide us from other brothers and sisters. It could be that some have a different vision, or perhaps we are jealous of the way God is blessing another's ministry. This must not happen. We must also recognize and repent of any prejudices against other nationalities.

I'm not talking about an ideal. This unity has been achieved in the Somebody Cares network. Unity, which has come about gradually, has accelerated since the mid-1990s. Let me tell you about one season in late 1996 that stands out in my memory as a manifestation of the many-hued but closely woven coat of many colors. It happened during the forty days of meetings called Houston Prayer Mountain.

UNITING FOR PRAYER AND WORSHIP

Although Houston rests on flat terrain, at one time, there was an amphitheater overlooking the city. It was built on a man-made hill at the intersection of two major highways. It became the setting of a significant gathering for the *Church in Houston*, so called because the book of Revelation, recorded by the apostle John, addresses the churches of the New Testament as being represented within their cities—the Church in Ephesus, the Church in Smyrna, and so on.

Great expectancy arose in the leaders of the church of Houston as we committed ourselves to join together for a time of corporate repentance and renewal. The first weekend of Houston Prayer Mountain took place in March 1996. We believed the timing was right for a major spiritual breakthrough in the city.

On the first day of Houston Prayer Mountain in November 1996, three hundred pastors and ministry leaders took communion together. We met for forty nights of prayer and worship. Many of us fasted. We left our differences behind and came together for a common purpose: to worship the Lord and pray for souls. Each night, the front of the meeting place was filled as people came forward and God cleansed their hearts. Services often lasted five to six hours or more.

On one particular evening, a time for reconciliation took place. Restoration of relationships was happening at many of the gatherings, but this night was especially memorable. We spontaneously began to ask the Lord to show us if there were any barriers among us—any prejudices or hurts between members of different races or denominations that we needed to release.

Ministry leaders began to embrace and pray for one another. Christian Arab hugged messianic Jew, and Jew embraced German. Chinese and Japanese leaders prayed for each other. Anglo and African-American sought each other out. Mainline denominational and nondenominational ministers joined together in the essentials of the faith. Black, yellow, red, white, and brown—a coat of many colors—was woven together that night. This was not planned; it was a spontaneous work of God's Spirit. What an awesome sight to witness the healing that took place!

As we brought together people from different denominations and backgrounds, we recognized a common denominator: a passion for God and compassion for souls.

As we brought together people from different denominations and backgrounds, we recognized a common denominator: a passion for God and compassion for souls. We all desired to see souls added to God's kingdom. We prayed and fasted for this purpose.

One evening, twenty-seven different nationalities attended the meeting. Drawn by the integration, many New Age people and others were saved.

Thirty different worship teams, representing various denominations, races, and cultures, eventually participated in Houston Prayer Mountain's praise and worship. The Lord blended the sounds into a sweet melody as inner-city ministries worshipped with those from suburban churches; frontline outreaches such as homeless shelters, AIDS ministries, inner-city youth ministries, and gang ministries all bridged their differences. The diversity was an expression of the beauty of the bride of Christ.

Not only did we agree on a common purpose—evangelism—but we took action. What good is it to develop new concepts if we don't move from theory to practice? In one day alone, we distributed 80,000 pounds of food at a citywide feeding event, cooperating with Goad International. At another event, in cooperation with Operation Blessing, we gave away groceries to 5,000 families.

After the original forty days of Houston Prayer Mountain, we gathered there again for five days around Easter weekend of 1997. Our final season of prayer at the amphitheater took place from December 26, 1997, and continued through February 1998. Then the owners of the facility closed it, and the hill upon which the amphitheater rested was leveled. Ironically, it was replaced with a tree and plant nursery—a permanent reminder of all the spiritual seeds that took root and sprouted among us during the Houston Prayer Mountain services.

The Lord humbled us and broke down many barriers during those days at Houston Prayer Mountain. Our time together was a small picture of what we read in Micah chapter four, as people gathered from various languages, nations, and denominations from across the city. We realized that God wants to wrap us with His love—His robe of righteousness—so that together, we can become a coat of many colors offered back to our Lord Jesus Christ. And He wants us to make a difference in the lives of others.

LAYING DOWN OUR LIVES AND PREJUDICES

When you and I put on Christ, we must also *"put on love"* (Colossians 3:14). Jesus displayed His love in dying for us *"while we were still sinners"* (Romans 5:8). He willingly chose to lay down His life for all nations, all peoples, and all cultures. We did not earn or deserve His love, but Christ chose to love us anyway.

> *Jesus willingly chose to lay down His life for all nations, all peoples, and all cultures. We did not earn or deserve His love, but He chose to love us anyway.*

Because He did that for us, whatever offenses or prejudices we hold must be released. Some of the unforgiveness we harbor may have been picked up from years past—within a particular church denomination, or with someone of a particular racial background—yet we must get past these offenses if we want to impact our communities.

Kenny desperately wanted to end an unfulfilling lifestyle in which he always craved something more, but was never satisfied. The men he lived with had money, expensive clothes, and luxury apartments. They threw parties with designer drugs, fine wines, and the best cuisine. Kenny struggled with his lust for that lifestyle, with its strings attached…and with his desire for the true freedom that he knew only came through Christ.

Years earlier, Kenny had been saved while in prison for robbery. He had committed the break-in to get money to pay bills, but had spent what he took on drugs. The youngest son of an abusive father, he had been molested by both male and female babysitters while growing up. His parents divorced, and then his father died. His mother moved in with an alcoholic whom Kenny hated. When he was fifteen, he became involved in drugs, which made it easy to experiment with homosexuality. The partying lifestyle took him straight to jail before he was out of his teens.

After his salvation in prison, Kenny never told anyone about his struggles. Upon his release, he served in a discipleship organization, his past firmly behind him. Then one night, Kenny found himself with a man and was shocked that he could fall so easily. He became discouraged and fell for the lie that he was missing out on something by having left his previous lifestyle. He left his ministry involvement and became a waiter at a restaurant with friends who seemed to promise the excitement he'd been missing.

One night, Deborah, a girl who had been witnessing to Kenny, took him to a Bible study at my apartment, and I met Kenny for the first time. He felt the tug to join us, but instead moved into a gay apartment complex, feeling that he was beyond help. One of his friends was an embezzler; together, they partied away the rewards of the embezzler's crime. I didn't see Kenny again for years.

Sometime later, Kenny decided to get an HIV test for his own peace of mind. The results were positive. The test results seemed like an official death notice, but Kenny's lifestyle had beaten the disease to the punch. He already felt dead inside. One lonely night, he lay on his couch and whispered, "Lord, it's obvious I can't run my life. Help me."

A few weeks later, he went out drinking with some friends when suddenly, sitting in a gay bar, he felt that he had to put down his beer and get out of there. When he walked outside, a Hispanic man from our ministry stopped Kenny to give him a tract. Having experienced discrimination himself, this man felt no discrimination against anyone who needed Jesus, no matter what lifestyle they were living. As a result, another life was saved.

There is a desperate need for healing in our land today. Our nation's citizens come from many cultural backgrounds; at times, there have been serious conflicts to overcome. In a similar way, those in the church come from different cultures, backgrounds, and neighborhoods, but we are one family with one common identity in Jesus Christ.

Within the Somebody Cares ministry, individuals represent many different nationalities and cultures. I thank the Lord for each one. At one time, we even had a worship team called *the Coat of Many Colors* because it was comprised of people from Asian, African-American, Jewish, Hispanic, and Anglo backgrounds. We did not seek to have a racially mixed group, but each one was drawn by having the same heart for the Lord and a desire to see souls added to His kingdom.

CROSSING EVERY BOUNDARY

Because the kingdom of God is transcultural, He may send you to another nation, or He may ask you to go across town to work with people of a different background. Are you willing to go where He leads you? When you think of reaching out to particular groups or neighborhoods, what fears come to mind? We use a variety of excuses for not reaching out to others. Perhaps these comments sound familiar:

- *I can't go into that neighborhood; they won't listen to me.*
- *You don't understand. I'm too old to talk with those people.*
- *I don't really want to go out in public with people like that.*
- *I can't talk to the checkout people at the supermarket, or they'll think I'm a freak.*

God is not limited by cultural, racial, or denominational backgrounds, *nor should we limit ourselves.* It's not a Hispanic thing, an Asian thing, an African thing, or an Anglo thing. It's a Jesus thing!

God wants to use us to penetrate every neighborhood and every heart for His kingdom. But first, we must deal with our own fears and prejudices and then make ourselves available. We could be the very ones to bring about healing and breakthrough for others.

> *God is not limited by cultural, racial,*
> *or denominational backgrounds,*
> *nor should we limit ourselves.*

TOGETHER ON FIRE

A picture hangs in my office: Jesus wearing a vibrant tunic covered with national flags from all over the world. On several occasions, in some measure, this picture became a reality in our city. One of those occasions was the Together on Fire gathering, which brought together different Asian ethnicities.

The gathering, coordinated by Joy Wang and assisted by Somebody Cares Houston pastors, was a breathtaking experience unprecedented in Houston history at the time. Both evenings began with a procession of national flags. Forming a circle at the altar, each minister bowed his flag as the cross of Christ was raised high above them all. We took communion together, acknowledging that though nations may have been divided in the past, they were now united through the gospel of Christ.

Across the front of the sanctuary, the national flags provided a backdrop for two extraordinary services. Pastors took the platform, displaying the beauty of their cultures through native costumes that represented the communities of Vietnamese, Chinese, Taiwanese, Japanese, Indian, Filipino, Korean, Indonesian, Hispanic, Jewish, and African peoples. Each prayed in his or her native tongue for revival in our city and in their homelands.

Houston was then second only to New York City for diversity of cultures and languages spoken. (In 2020, Houston was named most diverse city in America, surpassing the Big Apple.)

That first night, racial and cultural barriers fell as the church of Houston stood united to reach the lost. I had the privilege of sharing an evangelistic challenge both evenings, and many came to the altar to receive Christ. From teen to adult, lives were changed forever.

One of the Korean pastors said:

> I saw a definite awareness that our local church is not the end of our mission, but our mission is to see revival come to all nations. It was also a joy to hear the different prayers in their native languages, especially the Hebrew prayer. When the messianic rabbi prayed in Hebrew, I saw the Old and New Testaments come together, with the Old Testament being fulfilled in the New. It was awesome.

Think of the impact the church in any city will have if all races and denominations unify in order to win the lost! This is the Lord's desire and will bring great joy to His heart. Picture the threads of the coat blending into a tapestry of all national flags as we, Christ's church, become one body.

Houston missed out on a great visitation by God in the early years of the twentieth century. A black preacher named William Seymour came to Houston, but was not allowed to participate in the Bible classes except on the other side of a screen that separated the races. He eventually left Houston and went to Los Angeles, where he was instrumental in sparking the Azusa Street revival that reached millions. Because of racial prejudice, our city missed out on a visitation of God.

We believe that God wants to bring a mighty revival to the land, and we don't want to miss it. One of our slogans in the city is, "Give us Houston, give us the nations."

THE UNFINISHED COAT OF MANY COLORS?

Remember the story of the Hispanic man from our ministry who handed a tract to a man desperate to find a way out of his lifestyle? That one simple action eventually brought Kenny into God's kingdom to add his color to the robe. It took months to break down the walls Kenny had built in his life. But eventually, alone in his apartment, he reached out and touched his Bible for the first time in years. He knew how to repent and how to pray. That night, he felt life surge within him again. Soon, he joined us to grow and learn.

Kenny started taking missions trips to Mexico, Central and South America, and Europe. His HIV was slow to progress, and his strength was slow to fail. On his second trip to Germany, he fell in love with the German people, and he traveled there often, making a difference for Christ in that country. Who would have dreamed that handing a piece of paper to a man emerging from a bar was part of the Lord's plan to birth a missionary?

Where is God challenging you to go? To the streets? To your neighborhood? To the schools, the government, or to another nation? Find out where the people in your community are going. What do they do to deal with their hurts? Where do they run? We must follow them and identify their real needs so we can be instruments of God's healing.

Our faithfulness to the Lord today is an important step in fulfilling His long-range call on our lives. He has not finished weaving His coat of many colors. He will not be finished until every last soul has an opportunity to respond to the gospel. That is the challenge set before us.

5

MENDING THE NET

*He said to Simon, "Launch out into the deep and let down
your nets for a catch." But Simon answered and said to Him,
"Master, we have toiled all night and caught nothing; nevertheless at Your word I will let down the net." And when they
had done this, they caught a great number of fish, and their
net was breaking. So they signaled to their partners in the
other boat to come and help them. And they came and filled
both the boats, so that they began to sink.*
—Luke 5:4–7

Imagine the thoughts that went through Simon Peter's mind
when Jesus told him to cast his net again after a whole night of

catching no fish: *I've been working at this a long time. I've already put my net in the water but haven't caught anything. Why would the results be any different this time?*

Peter wrestled with his doubts, yet he obeyed Jesus and put the net in the water. Peter walked in faith, trusting that the Lord knew better than he did. Sure enough, the net was soon filled with fish. In fact, it was so full that Peter had to call his neighbors to help him.

What joy must have filled Peter's heart! Yet the event also left him shaken.

> *When Simon Peter saw it, he fell down at Jesus' knees, saying, "Depart from me, for I am a sinful man, O Lord!" For he and all who were with him were astonished at the catch of fish which they had taken.* (Luke 5:8–9)

The disciples' labor through the night is like our labor in the flesh. Very little is accomplished by our own efforts, but when the Lord directs us, that's when we see results. Jesus spoke the word; the disciples obeyed and then pulled in a multitude of fish.

Nothing is greater than seeing the hand of God intervene in a situation.

> *Like Peter, we are called to be fishers of men. There is no shortage of fish. Millions of people are waiting to be brought into the kingdom.*

Like Peter, we are called to be fishers of men. There is no shortage of fish. Millions of people are waiting to be brought into the kingdom. How can we bring in the greatest catch? We routinely cast our fishing hooks into the water—with friendship, evangelism, crusades, and church services—but we don't catch the greatest number of fish with those individual approaches. If our approach to fishing yields few results, or if the fish we catch do not stay caught, then it's time to change what we're doing.

A single fishing pole catches one fish at a time, but with a net, we can bring in many fish at once. Although we are called individually to a particular area of ministry, collectively, we are called to the world. As we tie our individual abilities and ministries together, we can bring in the catch God has prepared.

SPREAD, WASH, AND CAST THE NET

When Jesus first approached them, *"the fishermen had gone from them* [their boats] *and were washing their nets"* (Luke 5:2). To prepare for fishing, the nets were first spread out and then washed. Likewise, we must open our nets first by opening our hearts and allowing the Lord to cleanse us and deal with any issues—insecurities, fears, or hurts from the past—that hinder His work through us.

When Dennis and Mary came to our ministry meetings from another church, they were fearful of allowing themselves to hook up with us—or with any Christians, for that matter. I soon learned why. They had been part of the *shepherding movement*, which taught that people must have accountability to leadership. Taken to the extreme, as in their case, leaders and elders controlled every decision.

Mary had never trusted the leadership of the church, but Dennis believed they were good people who wanted to do right. After many years of being shepherded to the extent that others even told Dennis what job he could have and what car he could buy, one day, he learned of some financial misdealings in the leadership. He was crushed.

Mary had recently heard me talk at a Bible study about the church in Vietnam, and she was intrigued enough to suggest to Dennis that they come to hear me. Dennis felt apprehensive. He'd been so shattered that he believed he could never again be part of the body of Christ or trust anyone in church leadership.

When I heard their story, I urged Dennis and Mary to come and hang out with us, but I didn't ask them to do anything. You see, until the *net* of their lives had been spread out, opened up, and cleaned, there was no reason to put it to work in the boat. They weren't ready. But God's love and His Word worked over a period of time and they overcame their hurts and fears. Both Dennis and Mary experienced pain in the healing process, but it was also a time of building character.

It took them a while to get used to the fact that I wasn't going to tell them what to do. Instead, I was going to teach them how to hear God's voice for themselves. After many months, Dennis and Mary finally felt ready to jump into the boat and be part of the mended net for the church of Houston. When they did, they watched the Lord draw people to Himself.

A MENDED NET

After the nets are spread out and washed, they are placed back in the boat, ready to be used for the catch. Jesus instructed the disciples, "*Launch out into the deep and **let down your nets** for a catch*" (Luke 5:4).

Jesus used the word *nets* as if they had not one net but many. In the next verse, Peter agrees to "*let down **the net**,*" singular. Could it be that the fishermen had connected their nets into one large net? By faith, were they anticipating a great catch? They cast the net into the water, "*and when they had done this, they caught a great number of fish, and their net was breaking*" (verse 6).

When Peter and the disciples obeyed the Lord, the one net was neither large enough nor strong enough to hold all the fish. What were they to do? Their resources were limited, and they had nothing else with which to catch the fish. Peter had to act quickly, or they would lose the fish. *"So they signaled to their partners in the other boat to come and help them. And they came and filled both the boats, so that they began to sink"* (verse 7).

The disciples learned a valuable principle that day. They needed the help of other fishermen to bring in the catch. No single person, church, or ministry working alone can handle the harvest of souls the Lord desires to bring into His kingdom. Our focus is not on building individual kingdoms, but on building God's kingdom. To see His kingdom built, we must be willing to link our net with the nets of others for an even greater catch.

> *Our focus is not on building individual kingdoms, but on building God's kingdom.*

We who are fishers of men often face times of discouragement when it seems that the labor is in vain. Each of us goes through seasons when the fruit is hard to harvest, and we find ourselves tempted to go back to our old ways. After Jesus died, the disciples grieved their loss and went back to what they did before they met Him:

Simon Peter said to them, "I am going fishing." They said to him, "We are going with you also." They went out and immediately got into the boat, and that night they caught nothing.

(John 21:3)

Jesus appeared to them after the resurrection and instructed them:

"Cast the net on the right side of the boat, and you will find some." So they cast, and now they were not able to draw it in because of the multitude of fish....Simon Peter went up and dragged the net to land, full of large fish, one hundred and fifty-three; and although there were so many, the net was not broken.

(John 21:6, 11)

That's when the disciples worked together to drag the net to shore. As they combined their efforts, they successfully brought in the catch, and the net was not even torn. Many evangelistic ministries have been torn up while trying to draw in their nets, not realizing there is synergy and safety in partnering with others.

Scripture says that Peter and his friends in the neighboring boats brought in 153 fish, a number that theologians say represents the known nations at that time in history. Even by the number of fish caught, Jesus prophetically spoke to the disciples and to us with the message that we will make disciples of all peoples, tribes, tongues, and nations.

Though the disciples had gone back to fishing, Jesus was reminding them of their original calling: *"I will make you become fishers of men"* (Mark 1:17). The calling had never changed. Though circumstances spoke a contrary message, Jesus was telling them that His purpose would be fulfilled in their lives.

> *Though the night has been long and the catch has been small, God's plan never changes.*
> *He will instruct us how to bring in the harvest.*

The same is true for us. Though the night has been long and the catch has been small, God's plan never changes. He will instruct us how to bring in the harvest; and though the net is filled, it will not break. He will faithfully watch over us and assist us in becoming fishers of men.

As a result of Somebody Cares Houston linking nets for a greater catch, we are reaching the community at a grassroots level. We maintain our distinctiveness and our individual callings, but we recognize that we need to work together to see a vast number of people reached. This takes some doing, but the work is so worthwhile that the time involved and the price paid cannot be compared to the joy of seeing lives changed by Christ.

Although God is already doing a great work within separate ministries, the next step is to link the ministries together to become part of something bigger than ourselves. As we become a mended net, even with our diversities and our distinctiveness, we can reach a greater harvest.

UNITED WE STAND

God has a plan for each of us once we are cleaned, mended, and ready to link with others. Dennis and Mary eventually interned at a children's ministry in Tulsa for two years, then they returned to Houston and worked with our ministry to children, including outreach to children of our community through Somebody Cares. Upon graduation, several churches and ministries offered them lucrative jobs, which they turned down to return to Houston. Dennis and Mary wanted to serve as missionaries to the children under the umbrella of Somebody Cares, and they have remained focused and faithful to that calling.

Jesus reminded the disciples of their first calling and responsibility when He told them they would be fishers of men. That's what we are, too. As we cast our nets and work with our neighbors, we will have the greatest possible catch without breaking the net. A true network is a net that works.

6

UNITY WITH A PURPOSE

"Jerusalem shall be inhabited as towns without walls,
because of the multitude of men and livestock in it.
For I," says the LORD, *"will be a wall of fire all around her,*
and I will be the glory in her midst."
—Zechariah 2:4–5

T he young man, drenched with water, laid his head on Pastor Ernie Lopez's shoulder and embraced him. He had found hope and newness of life that day and the baptism sealed the work God had done. His was one of many testimonies that came out of a citywide baptism held at an entertainment water park. Water park officials said we had a record attendance of 4,100 people. This was another memorable day for Houston as denominational and racial walls came down for a common focus. We were united for a purpose that would have eternal consequences.

Richard Hinojosa, a youth pastor of the Encourager Church at the time, and I preached from a platform in the wave pool. Over one hundred churches took part, and close to fifty pastors representing many denominations and ethnicities helped to baptize over 600 people.

One pastor knelt down in the water as he prayed for a young boy before baptizing him. Some jumped out of the water filled with joy. Young adults committed to walk radically and boldly in purity with Christ. One young teen raised his arms, fists clenched, giving a victory punch as he rose from the water. A woman shook her arms in praise as she was baptized.

Small prayer huddles comprised of young and old joined hands and prayed with the same heart cry. Throughout the baptisms, individuals continued to ask for prayer to receive Christ. By conservative estimates, 200 people made first-time commitments or rededications to Christ.

That day spiritual chains broke off people's lives and the battle was won for souls! Of the shades of black, white, yellow, and brown, only one color was seen that day—blood red! You could sense the freedom and victory Jesus brought.

Local television networks filmed and reported the citywide baptism. Our local NBC station reported, "Hundreds of Houstonians turned out for a big baptism at Adventure Bay Water Theme Park. Houston area pastors and ministers from various denominations did the honors for this celebration of Christian faith." The historic impact of the day came from the power of God and was far beyond anything we had imagined.

IT IS VERY GOOD

The work each ministry is sowing into our city is good. But when we unite, the results go beyond good to tremendous.

During Houston Prayer Mountain, Pastor Glenn Carter, who served on the Somebody Cares Houston advisory committee, was a guest on a local television station. He shared about his involvement in Somebody Cares and explained how each participating ministry is important to God. He made a parallel between our networking of ministries and the creation story from Genesis: *"And God saw that it was good....Then God saw everything that He had made, and indeed it was very good"* (Gen. 1:10, 31).

After day one, God looked at His creation and said, "It is good." After the sixth day, He looked at His creation and said, "It is *very* good."

Reflecting on Pastor Glenn's comments, I, too, believe that the Father looks at each denomination, each inner-city ministry, and each suburban church, and says, "It is good." Yet as we work together with a common purpose, I sense Him saying, "It is very good." Individually each ministry is good and is doing a good work. But as one united body, we are effective in bringing in a great harvest that is pleasing to the Father.

When I was having lunch one day with my friend Jim Herrington, former director of Mission Houston, he said, "The reason I can be a part of Somebody Cares is because you've never asked me to give up my personal distinction."

The leaders in Houston appreciate each other's distinctiveness and the manner in which the Lord is using each individual or ministry to build His kingdom. No one asks others to give up their individual callings. That is why Somebody Cares works. Synergy takes place in the presence of a noncompetitive servant attitude that desires to build the Lord's kingdom as opposed to man's kingdom. We each bring what we have to the table and see what the Lord would have us do.

> *Synergy takes place in the presence of a noncompetitive servant attitude that desires to build the Lord's kingdom.*

When Jim was interviewed by the *Houston Chronicle* in 1996 for an article about Somebody Cares, he told them that the network is bringing together "a broad range of ministries who are touching people that traditional churches are not touching. It is street people, teenagers, and young people who don't find traditional church to have any meaning for them. Moreover, [we are] successfully reflecting the worldwide trend of churches and ministries to unite or cooperate for more effective ministry."

This is the purpose of the Somebody Cares unity. We do not advocate ecumenical unity, which is merely unity for unity's sake. Rather, we unite with a purpose.

REACHING OUT TO BRING THEM IN

Working together is the start. Gaining a shared vision for your city is the next step. Your ability to make an impact is directly related to how much you love your city and how much you believe God wants to do great things there.

Ethel Dunn was an African-American woman who provided a homeless shelter in downtown Houston called God's Little Lighthouse. When God got hold of her heart, Ethel sold her business in Alaska and moved to Houston to help the needy. She became involved in Somebody Cares through Houston Prayer Mountain and the ministers she met there. As relationships grew, some ministries offered to help at the shelter. Churches provided volunteers. Others provided workers and supplies to remove six layers of shingles and put on a new roof. Not only was Ethel's ministry blessed, but everyone who served with her was enriched. She went to be with Jesus in 2008.

Before retiring, Ray Highfield was founder and director of His Touch Ministries, a home for those with HIV and AIDS. Our hearts went out to Ray and his staff as they provided care and counseling every single day to residents and those who called. We were privileged to join His Touch Ministries for a Concert of Praise in which other area churches provided workers and raised community awareness. Ray traveled extensively, teaching AIDS awareness and prompting Christian communities nationwide to create outreaches to those affected by AIDS in their communities. The church becomes the tangible extension of Christ's love as we address serious needs.

THE AMAZING FRUIT OF SYNERGY

What would it be like if the churches and ministries in your city worked together in a network similar to that of Somebody Cares, not just for a specific project but as a long-term commitment? Your city would never be the same. This is more than a theory— it has been tested and proven in our ongoing experience in Houston. It has spread to Tampa Bay, Baltimore, New England, St. Augustine, Denver, San Antonio, and elsewhere around the nation and the world.

One year, we distributed over 150,000 Somebody Cares New Testaments throughout the city of Houston, plus the Spanish equivalent, Alguien Se Interesa. In 1996, 40 million pounds of food were distributed by Action Ministries, working in conjunction with Somebody Cares. In 1997, that figure rose to 102 million pounds of food. By 1999, 115 million pounds of food were distributed! Action Ministries remained a partner for many years, meeting needs of thousands in our city.

At Christmastime a few years ago, someone gave us retail space in one of the local malls and we distributed 10,600 toys to underserved children who were able to take a trip to the mall to pick out their Christmas presents just like more advantaged children. We created several hundred Somebody Cares bears for this outreach, which was the most coveted toy of all. These little plush white bears wore T-shirts bearing the same message as the business card: "A true witness rescues lives." We now distribute these bears to children who have been affected by natural disasters or gone through other traumas.

One year, we rotated a billboard around the city with the message "Area churches and ministries want you to know Somebody Cares Houston." Another year, we partnered with Christian Broadcasting Network to distribute over a half million copies of *Book of Hope*. We distributed prayer door hangers to more than one million homes. We also obtained the rights to air the movie *Resurrection* for one year and aired it on both secular and Christian television stations.

Synergy works wherever people are willing to unite. In the year 2000, one of our chapters:

- Distributed over $4 million worth of food and mobilized thousands of prayer warriors statewide
- Worked with a dozen communities to air the *Jesus* video and taught hundreds of volunteers on evangelism
- Coordinated youth prayer events and conducted Care Days in needy areas with live music, free food, and ministry
- Distributed roughly 60,000 toys at Christmastime
- Networked with national ministries and coordinated with hundreds of local churches

Unseen things done for the kingdom are just as important in helping the overall effort to reach the lost. One night, while ministering at an inner-city church, I had the privilege of meeting a woman who has been praying for revival in our city for more than twenty years. God has heard her prayers. He honors those hours she and so many like her have spent on their knees and the tears they have wept for souls. They have prepared the way for revival.

> God honors those hours we spend on our knees in prayer and the tears we weep for souls.

A HUNGER FOR REVIVAL

As we work together and pray for each other, we increasingly recognize that we do not represent individual ministries but the body of Christ in our city. In Houston, during our meetings for pastors and leaders, we take the opportunity to pray for ministers who are coming into the city or are being sent out from the city. In this way, we acknowledge as city elders that we will cover them in prayer in addition to the covering of their local church and give them a corporate blessing from the church of Houston.

One couple received a vision at Houston Prayer Mountain and left our ministry to serve in Asia, so several Houston pastors prayed over them. As the elders of the city, we sent them out with a blessing and covering. Another minister had served as an associate pastor of a local church, then was asked to become the senior pastor. First, we blessed the pastor who was leaving the position and prayed for continued fruitfulness and favor in his life, and then we prayed for the new pastor and his wife. On behalf of the church of Houston, we received them into their new position. In such ways, we endeavor to serve the local congregation and further its ties with the body of Christ in our city.

Ultimately, we are representing Christ. But wherever the Lord may send us, we are also representing the church of our city. We want to be ambassadors about whom the Lord and others will give a good report.

Pastor Lopez, who worked with us at the baptism, has since expanded his men's and women's homes, moved into new facilities, strengthened their work to gang members, and has become a regional pastor for the Victory Outreach churches in the area. Picture him with the other ministers at one of our monthly Somebody Cares Houston meetings. He arrives along with the young and the old, every race and denomination, those helping the homeless, ex-convicts, recovering addicts, unwed moms, and street kids.

At such meetings, we come together to seek the Lord for revival in our communities, our city, and our nation. The love of God transcends our differences, and warm fellowship envelopes us as we discuss strategies to reach our city. We minister to one another, share our individual visions, and present practical needs. We feel privileged to serve alongside men and women who are making a difference in people's lives. We appreciate each other, but none of us wants to be the other. We don't compete for another's ministry.

SPARKS FROM HOUSTON

Several years ago, I envisioned the outpouring God desires to bring to our city and the world. I saw little flickers of flames, representing the intercessors, the churches, and the Christian communities that have been praying for revival. The flickers of flame lit across the greater Houston area and, as a wind began to blow, the flickers spread into a huge fire. From that fire, embers went out across the nation and to other countries. As God's Spirit blows through the city, the impact on Houston will spread outward to the nations.

Flames of revival and renewal are meant to rekindle that which has died. Do we hunger and thirst for God's righteousness to consume us and then sweep across our land?

God desires to burn a fire that ignites flames of revival in our cities. Like a raging forest fire, these revival flames will become uncontrollable. They will not be isolated to a particular area but will engulf the entire nation. *"'For I,' says the LORD, 'will be a wall of fire all around her, and I will be the glory in her midst'"* (Zechariah 2:5). God's revival flames form a wall of protection; they refine as well as consume. Before the flames can go outward to consume our enemies, they must purify us, lest we, too, be consumed.

Toward the end of the forty days on Houston Prayer Mountain, it was clear that something significant and unprecedented had taken place. Many requested we keep the meetings going, yet God spoke to me through another surprising vision. I saw a huge mountain, representing Houston Prayer Mountain, and then I saw a huge body of water, which represented the city of Houston. The mountain crumbled and disappeared into the water, and as it did, the water level rose. I sensed that God was saying the mountain would die so the spiritual water level would rise throughout the city.

On the last night of Houston Prayer Mountain, we held a candlelight prayer service to act out physically what we saw spiritually. The flickers of candlelight represented the saints who have prayed to the Lord of the harvest. The little flickers united spread the flames of God's fire.

Instead of just a centralized revival, the Lord wants the sparks of revival to set churches ablaze in every area of the city. We are now beginning to see a dynamic taking place that is indeed drawing people from other cities and nations. God is blowing His wind to ignite our flickers into revival flames.

Commenting on Houston Prayer Mountain, Steve Riggle, pastor of Grace Church and president of Grace International, said:

Prayer Mountain was a catalyst for our city in revival, at least in my estimation. Our church is radically changed;

the focus of our church and outreaches has changed considerably. I think of what will take place, not knowing how the whole process will unfold. But I believe what we've seen so far is just a small beginning.

THE BLUE HEELERS: A MODERN-DAY PARABLE

Hank Marion, pastor of New Haven House of Prayer, served on our Somebody Cares Houston steering committee and traveled with us to other cities to communicate the vision and strategies of Somebody Cares. He tells this story that illustrates the message of unity with a purpose:

> My dad has property in East Texas with 100 cows. Three times a year, all the cows are gathered into a corral to receive care. The process of getting the cows into the corral is not easy. Cows are not like dogs and cats that come running when you call them. In fact, they seem to sense when we are having a roundup and run to the far side of the ranch.
>
> My dad's friend has blue heelers, which are called "cow dogs." They are bred and trained to herd the cows into the corral. Whenever possible, we contact our friend with the dogs to get him involved in our roundup. Typically, at 7 a.m., we gather at the corral and greet each other while sharing stories and sipping coffee. At the appropriate time, the owner of the blue heelers will walk over to the cages and open the doors, while giving a shout: "Go get 'em."
>
> Like lightning, those dogs take off. This is what they live for, and nothing keeps them from the task. Across the pasture they bolt and surround the cows. Then with precision and teamwork, they bring the cows up the hill through all the gates and into the corral.

One time, another friend who lives just up the road was planning his own roundup. He knew about the blue heelers and invited them to come and work his cows, but there was one problem: instead of 100 cows, this man had about 500 cows. The owner of the blue heelers knew this was too much for his dogs to handle, but he had three friends who also had blue heelers. They decided they would all bring their dogs over on roundup day.

So there we were about 7 a.m., and it came time to let the dogs out. The owners did just that, but much to our surprise, the dogs ran to each other instead of taking off after the cows. They walked around each other sniffin' and snarlin' and checking each other out. Their masters were yelling at the top of their voices, "Blue, git on," and "Beau, stop it now." But it wasn't until the dogs decided everything was okay that they ran down the hill into the pasture and brought the cows into the pen.

The Lord has a big job for us to do. The harvest He has planned is so huge that it is going to require the whole church to accomplish it. He desires that we work together instead of separately. We must get past the sniffin' and snarlin' and become comfortable with one another. Otherwise, when the job is at hand and the work has begun, we will waste precious time.

We have to look at the need in the field—the mighty harvest waiting—and get over the sniffin' and snarlin' and growlin'. We must humble ourselves and work together to build God's kingdom.

7

PRAYING AND FASTING
WITH A PURPOSE

Is this not the fast that I have chosen: to loose the bonds of wick-
edness, to undo the heavy burdens, to let the oppressed go free,
and that you break every yoke? Is it not to share your bread
with the hungry, and that you bring to your house the poor who
are cast out; when you see the naked, that you cover him, and
not hide yourself from your own flesh? Then your light shall
break forth like the morning, your healing shall spring forth
speedily, and your righteousness shall go before you; the glory of
the LORD shall be your rear guard. Then you shall call, and the

LORD *will answer; you shall cry, and He will say, "Here I am."*
—Isaiah 58:6–9

The "fried chicken bandit" spent a total of eight months in the free world between Christmas 1969 and July 1985. Bob was charged with armed robbery of a Kentucky Fried Chicken store, aggravated assault, possession of heroin, felony theft, and a dozen other charges that put him in jail three different times. Each time he was released, he returned within four months.

During what would become Bob's final prison sentence, his drug-addicted brother, Ray, stumbled into a Christian bookstore in search of help. One of my spiritual sons, Randy Flinn, felt God tell him to go help a man in that same Christian bookstore. Just as Ray was looking at a row of Bibles and silently praying, "God if you are real, I need a sign," Randy walked up and said, "Do you need some help?"

After Ray's conversion, Bob was released from prison. He had met the Lord years earlier at a prayer meeting during the "Jesus freak" movement and had thrown his drugs out the car window of a friend, whose brother had taken them to the prayer meeting. But none of the three continued to follow Christ.

A friend took Bob to a church and to a Narcotics Anonymous meeting, but Bob wasn't going to return to Christ easily. For eight years, he screamed, cussed, and growled at people in his NA and Alcoholics Anonymous meetings. He was diagnosed with manic depression, but the prescribed drugs couldn't control him. He didn't want to go to prison again, so he stayed off drugs and alcohol, but continued to struggle with his thoughts and emotions.

At a checkup during a hot July day in 1992, Bob's doctor told him he'd be on lithium for the rest of his life—news that sent him to the breaking point. When he drove his truck away from the doctor's office, he thought he heard a page and called a number on his pager.

"Can I help you?" he asked the person on the other line, indicating to the listener that he was answering his pager.

"I didn't page anyone," said a man's voice.

"Well, I'm a roofing contractor. Is there anything I can do for you?"

"Well, I'm a pastor, and I lead people to the Lord. Is there anything I can do for you?"

Bob doesn't remember the man's prayer, but he remembers going to his AA meeting that night and telling them God had called him on the telephone that day.

A friend from AA invited him to one of our Bible studies, and that night, Bob responded to the altar call. Bob now says that I gave him the creeps that night—meaning the presence of the Holy Spirit was making him uncomfortable. He came up to me after the service and said, "You must be saying something pretty heavy because I can't understand a word of it." I just responded, "Keep coming."

His AA friend then took Bob to a local church, and that is where the breakthrough came. Bob believed that since he'd been saved years earlier, he didn't need to answer the call for salvation. But something during the altar call stirred him inside. He started to shake. The pastor said, "There's one more person who should answer the call tonight, and if you don't, you're going to regret it tomorrow."

Bob's first thought was to run out of the church, but instead he went to the front. As the pastor prayed with those at the altar, he said to Bob, "Tell Satan to leave you."

"Please leave me," Bob said.

"No, command him," the pastor said.

Bob didn't need a lot of encouragement to get angry. He shocked the entire church when he started screaming, "In the name of Jesus, get out of me NOW!"

The next time Bob entered one of our meetings, I could see the difference in him immediately. He was not only saved, he was delivered.

The Lord desires that none should perish but that all would come to the saving knowledge of His Son, Jesus Christ. (See 2 Peter 3:9.) He cares for the lost and wants to use us to lead them to a relationship with Him. Wimpy prayers won't bring deliverance to those enslaved by Satan. We must pray—individually and corporately—and pray with a purpose, asking, "God, what would You have me do?"

> *Wimpy prayers won't bring deliverance to those enslaved by Satan. We must pray—individually and corporately— and pray with a purpose.*

The two friends with whom Bob was originally saved as a young man returned to Christ, one in his final days before dying of AIDS. God desires to save and deliver every prison inmate, drug addict, and hopeless case. Our part is to pray for them.

WALLS COME DOWN

The late Dr. Edwin Louis Cole said, "We become intimate with the One to whom we pray, the one with whom we pray, and the one for whom we pray." From our place of intimacy with God, we become sensitive to His heart and His concerns, and we become intimate with others.

No evangelism can take place without a foundation of prayer. More than pious religious incantations, the prayer we need to pray is one of desperate, heartrending, passionate intercession. Missionary John Hyde modeled this when he cried out to God, "Give me souls or I die!" It was also exemplified by Bob Pierce, founder of World Vision, who prayed, "Break my heart with the things that break Yours."

Many avenues exist for individual and corporate prayer. I found one while seeking the Lord for His strategy in the early 1980s. I felt directed to the book of Joshua, and as I read about Joshua's march around the walled city of Jericho, something lit up inside me. Though the concept was not popular at the time, a group of us implemented Jericho marches around the environs of Houston and specifically at secular rock concerts. Today, some refer to these marches as prayer walks.

We would walk and pray in advance of the concerts, distributing gospel tracts and ministering one-on-one as we walked and prayed. Many were added to the kingdom as a result—some of whom are still working with us today.

After one concert, one young man wrote, "I read your Iron Maiden tract and said the prayer. It changed my life completely. I am asking for more tracts. Anything y'all have got I will pass around."

At another concert, a young woman was sick, and a group of young men were trying to take advantage of her. I challenged them, saying they were wimps, because real men would help her. Our group took her to the hospital, cared for her, and led her to Christ. At the next concert, we were again witnessing outside when a young woman approached us to say she was hoping we'd be there. She had watched us help the sick woman at the previous concert and wanted to know about God.

Years later, at a church service, a young man approached me and said he was one of the young punks harassing the sick woman at that concert. He said he and his friends had intended to beat me up, but they were so intimidated when I called them wimps that they stood there just trying to maintain their dignity. Later he found a church and gave his heart to Christ.

> *Evangelism and prayer go hand in hand.*
> *Prayer is fundamental to our relationship with God,*
> *but from that place of prayer,*
> *we move to a place of action.*

Evangelism and prayer go hand in hand. Prayer is fundamental to our relationship with God, but from that place of prayer, we move to a place of action. Evangelism is a natural result of our relationship with God.

JERICHO DRIVES

Joshua and the Israelites set a precedent for us when they marched around the walls of Jericho. (See Joshua 6.) They obeyed the Lord's instruction and trusted Him to bring down the walls of the city.

In 1988, some Houston-area ministers asked me what I thought was the next step for the city. We discussed strategies to pull down barriers within the church and see our city won for Christ. Though many wanted to see breakthroughs, it was clear that action was needed first within the church if we were to see walls in the community come down. The pastors agreed that a Jericho drive and rally could bring an initial breakthrough in the body of Christ as well as in the city.

The first Jericho drive was held May 7, 1988. We drove seven times around a highway that encircles the city, praying against specific strongholds. We culminated the drive with a prayer rally. The Jericho drives continued annually for four years and they continue to occur spontaneously to this day. When they took place, once a day for six days, we took turns driving around the highway that encircles the city. On the seventh day, we sometimes drove around the highway in shifts. But on the seventh time around, the entire group caravanned together, praying for souls. Each drive ended with a praise rally at a local church.

Some area pastors now conduct all-night prayer meetings that conclude with a Jericho drive for the city.

What seemed radical at the time are now common events worldwide. Intercessors and community prayer leaders frequently call for prayer walks and prayer drives exactly like the Jericho drive we once did more out of inspiration than organization.

One prayer walk in particular stands out in my mind. Pastor Kendall Bridges, who pastors now in the Dallas-Fort Worth area, felt called to fast for personal and corporate revival. In his own words, here is what happened:

> What started as a ten-day fast was extended to twenty-one days and then to forty days. A few men from our church joined me. After the fast, I experienced personal revival and we experienced revival in our church. A new depth of consecration developed. But I realized that if we want citywide revival, it is going to take consistent consecration and consistent sacrifice. We often make commitments leading up to special events, then go back to mediocrity afterward. Each of us has to make a deeper commitment. So, how bad do we want it?

In addition to the fast, God called those men and myself to a Jericho Walk for our city. We began at 8 p.m. one Friday night and walked the 610 Loop around downtown Houston, about a forty-mile walk. The next week, God moved on my heart to do another Jericho Walk around a larger loop, Beltway 8, which is almost ninety miles. In preparation, I faxed area churches and ministries and asked for their prayer requests, and we lifted those needs to the Lord while we walked.

The walk took four days, averaging twenty miles per day. We held nightly services, and I asked a different minister to share the Word each night. Ministers from Asian, Hispanic, and African-American backgrounds participated. If we want to keep seeing revival, we must continue to sacrifice. Though I am not much into walking, getting out there and being alone with God was wonderful.

John and Debbie Ojeda were saved through our ministry in 1996 and now have a ministry to the biker community called Prodigals Redeemed. During one of my weekly teachings, I talked about the Jericho drives.

When the teaching ended, John asked, "Can we do a Jericho ride with motorcycles?"

I responded, "Yes, you sure can!"

The first Jericho ride was in 2009 with about twelve riders circling the city of Houston on the Interstate 610 freeway, praying over the city. The next Jericho ride grew to eight cities in Texas, with about twenty-five riders in Houston. By 2013, the Jericho ride consisted of 103 cities around the world: ninety-eight in the U.S., two in Canada, two in Scotland, and one in Ireland. The numbers increased nearly every year they facilitated the rides.

In addition to prayer rides, drives, and walks, we have also had ongoing organized prayer for our city. As their part in Somebody Cares, Pastor Emeritus Richard Shearer's staff at Bammel Baptist Church implemented a prayer activity called Occupy the Land. On a grid map of Houston, the city's 2,700 square miles were broken into half-mile square sectors. Individuals from dozens of churches adopted various segments for which they committed to pray each day. Over 75 percent of this area was covered by daily prayer. To have people praying for their neighborhoods daily is a major commitment, but it is a vital part of the harvest in our city.

DISCERNING SPIRITUAL STRONGHOLDS

In 1988, during the first Jericho drive, the late Pastor Mike Cave shared a message that is still pertinent today:

> The changes taking place in cities today will either move them toward more evil and more corruption, or else something will intervene to reverse the trend and move the cities toward godliness. Whoever takes the lead in these major mega-centers of our world is going to affect the course of history....People are drawn to the city with a false hope of security in jobs, in commerce, and in all the things they mistakenly assume [it] will provide for them. In reality, the spirit of the city is nothing but a web that draws people into its clutches. The church must intercede and cry out to God for mercy.

Because of the variety and number of people in Houston, there exists a variety of strongholds, including pride, greed, violence, moral impurity, and a spirit of control that rebels against God's authority. An independent mentality has hindered the church in our city and throughout the body of Christ in America. For that reason, getting churches and ministries to work together is a difficult process. Yet breakthroughs have come as area ministry leaders have co-labored for the sake of the lost.

One thing I always teach is a basic principle anyone can carry with them to any church, ministry, or mission field in which they serve: *While men reach for thrones to build their own kingdoms, Jesus reached for a towel to wash men's feet.* We must have a servant's heart toward each other and toward this generation. Only with this sacrificial attitude will we see the needed breakthroughs in the church and in our cities, and souls added to God's kingdom.

> *While men reach for thrones to build their own kingdoms, Jesus reached for a towel to wash men's feet. We must have a servant's heart toward each other.*

REBUILDING SPIRITUAL WALLS

Prayer is not just talking to God; it is listening to His voice and being ready to obey. As we develop an intimate relationship with the Lord and with each other, we receive His corporate instruction to reach our communities and follow through with action.

We have more people praying for revival in America today than ever before. We are crying out to God and claiming His promise:

> *If My people who are called by My name will humble themselves, and pray and seek My face, and turn from their wicked ways, then I will hear from heaven, and will forgive their sin and heal their land.*   (2 Chronicles 7:14)

Yet we often forget the requirement Isaiah gave us to reach outward to the needy in addition to reaching upward to God. When we commit ourselves to seeking both upward and outward, nothing can stop revival.

Then your light shall break forth like the morning, your healing shall spring forth speedily, and your righteousness shall go before you; the glory of the LORD shall be your rear guard.
(Isaiah 58:8)

John R. Mott was a great Protestant statesman and a 1946 Nobel laureate. Understanding the power of evangelism when combined with social action, Mott once remarked, "Evangelism without social work is deficient; social work without evangelism is impotent." Separating these two components of effective outreach has been a tragic mistake of much of our evangelism in the past century.

God wants the spiritual walls of our city rebuilt, but this means more than devising an elaborate spiritual infrastructure; the real issue is rebuilding the lives of people shattered by the consequences of sin.

Bob Camp, the fried chicken bandit, became an integral part of our ministry. For years, he led services in prisons and helped with pastoral care for new converts coming out of drug and alcohol problems.

HE WILL COME WHERE WE GO

Jesus made a great promise to the disciples. As He commissioned them to go out two by two, He promised that if they would go, He would go with them to every city and place He sent them. (See Luke 10:1.)

God is about to move like we have never seen before. But we must be faithful to go where He sends us. Are we willing to make the sacrifices? Will we be laborers to help in the mighty harvest of souls? Are we willing to work with believers of different ethnic groups or different denominations to reach our cities? Will we say yes to whatever it takes?

The Lord wants to send you and me ahead of Him to prepare the way for His coming. Wherever we set our feet to go, His tangible presence will be there. Whether we go into the neighborhood streets or to a foreign field, the result will be the same: if we are faithful to go where He leads, He will show up in a powerful way.

> Whether we go into the neighborhood streets
> or to a foreign field, if we are faithful to
> go where God leads,
> He will show up in a powerful way.

If we are going to reach this generation, we must do more than just get together for fellowship and prayer. Yes, prayer is foundational, but we must pray with purpose. Fasting helps us die to our flesh, but we must fast with purpose.

The prophet Isaiah clarified the purpose for times of prayer and fasting. The Lord told him:

> Is not this the kind of fasting I have chosen: to **loose the chains of injustice** and untie the cords of the yoke, to **set the oppressed free** and break every yoke? Is it not to share your food with the hungry and to provide the poor wanderer with shelter—when you see the naked, to clothe them, and not to turn away from your own flesh and blood? Then your light

*will break forth like the dawn, and **your healing will quickly appear.*** (Isaiah 58:6–8 NIV)

Are you ready to move from passive prayer and fasting to justice in action?

8

PRAY UNTIL SOMETHING HAPPENS

Be in pain, and labor to bring forth, O daughter of Zion,
like a woman in birth pangs.
—Micah 4:10

Randy's overbearing, abusive father wounded him deeply as a child. Spankings always turned into beatings. Irritation usually turned into rage. At a young age, Randy would retreat to his bedroom to escape reality by exercising his artistic imagination in dance. During his teens, his dance abilities became a form of identity and a way to receive affirmation. He won championships and soon earned a name for himself as a rising star.

By his early twenties, Randy's dance troupe was an opening act for major concerts and he worked for radio stations and nightclubs. But the life of professional dancing was a nightmare for him. Inside the studio, dancers forced their bodies to perform; outside, they destroyed their bodies with eating disorders, drug addictions, and dangerous sexual relationships. Addicted to the accolades brought on by performance, Randy lived from show to show, waiting for the next applause, waiting to be "discovered," and living between shows in misery. Randy could never outrun the horrid feelings left over from the sick relationship he had experienced with his father.

Randy came to my old fitness studio and offered to swap aerobics instruction for studio time to rehearse his dance troupe. I had just prayed my agonizing prayer in the back room to make myself available to God, and I welcomed Randy wholeheartedly. One of the first evenings he was there, he came to church with me and gave his heart to the Lord, and immediately took to the streets with me to witness.

At the time, it was a bizarre concept to dance inside a church building, but as God reconstructed Randy in spirit, soul, and body, he had a growing idea that he might be able to use his gift of dance to help further the kingdom. Randy ministered where he was, but prayed in earnest for the chance to dance for the Lord. Like Henry Ford, who first built cars and then had to build roads on which to drive them, Randy now had to pray for churches in which he could exercise his gift. Randy *prayed*.

As we walked the streets, worked out physically, and lived by faith financially, prayer proved to be a more valuable lesson than anything else we ever learned.

As we walked the streets, worked out physically, and lived by faith financially, prayer proved to be a more valuable lesson than anything else we ever learned. We didn't know what to do when demon-possessed people lunged at us, or when we found out we'd brought home someone who had just overdosed…but we did learn how to pray. We didn't know how we'd pay the bills or feed the hungry people all around us, but we learned how to pray until something happened.

In 1997, Edwin Louis Cole spoke at Prayer Mountain. He saw a banner we'd hung that read, "P.U.S.H. (Pray Until Something Happens)" and commented, "That sounds like a woman in labor." I thought about it for a moment and realized that's exactly what it meant! God wants to birth something through us.

Any woman who has experienced childbirth understands the perseverance and strength required. Most women would say the pain is excruciating. But as intense as the labor pains are, great joy comes with the first glimpse of the infant. Words cannot describe the love, thankfulness, and peace experienced by a mother and father after a safe delivery.

The process is no different when laboring for God's kingdom. The pain is intense and the hours of labor are often long—but, oh, the joy that comes with each soul's birth into the kingdom!

> *When laboring for God's kingdom, the pain is intense and the hours of labor are often long—but, oh, the joy that comes with each soul's birth into the kingdom!*

I once heard an evangelist say, "With one ear we listen to the sweet melodies of heaven, and with the other ear, we hear the cries of hell." We live inside an intense battle raging over people's souls. The Spirit of the Lord is upon us to preach good news, liberty, and healing, and we have been commissioned by the Lord to share this message. (See Isaiah 61:1–2.) Like a woman travailing in labor, we must pray through the birthing process for the souls who have not yet responded to the gospel.

God alone knows what it will take to turn a heart toward Him. He gives us the privilege to pray with perseverance for someone's soul. Even when things don't seem to be happening, we must look on the situation with eyes of faith and not gaze on the natural circumstances. We must trust the Lord's wisdom because He alone knows the things He is working out in someone's life.

BURNING UP THE DROSS

Many Christians today are praying for a move of God that will impact thousands of souls and bring revival to our nation. But if we believe God is going to move, we have to prepare our own hearts. We must examine our own lives and allow Him to show us the things in us that are displeasing to Him.

Who are we when no one else is looking? It is what we do behind closed doors, where no one else can see us, that determines the power of God or lack of it in public. We must be the same people in our prayer closets as we are in public prayer meetings.

> *We must be the same people in our prayer closets as we are in public prayer meetings.*

In times at the altar, many of us pray for God's holy fire to consume us, but I am not sure we know what we're asking for. Have the flames become so intense that the only thing left burning within us is holy hunger for Him? Has the fire of God ignited a burning passion within us for His purposes? That is the Lord's desire. As we examine what those revival flames actually do, our lives will be changed and our prayers will ascend to God as a sweet aroma.

God is going to burn out the dross in our lives, and He is going to shake all that can be shaken. Hebrews 12 addresses this type of shaking and goes on to tell us to offer acceptable worship to God, with reverence and awe *"for our God is a consuming fire"* (verse 29). Acceptable worship to the Lord requires a heart that honors Him.

Simple obedience is one of the highest forms of worship. God is looking for people who have an obedient, sacrificial servant's heart. We must walk with humility and a fear of the Lord. Only that is acceptable worship and is pleasing in His sight. Once our hearts are broken before Him, He can consume us with His flames and make us catalysts for revival in others.

PRAYING THROUGH FOR BREAKTHROUGH

For a time, Randy struggled to leave behind his old reasons for dance to become pure in heart and gain his acceptance and approval from the applause of heaven, not from man. He struggled to overcome the bitterness toward his father that slumbered in an easy chair in his heart. As he prayed, he pushed—and things began to happen. First, Randy became a new creation in Christ. Then churches started changing their ways to embrace the idea of dance ministry, and doors began to fly open for him. When the breakthrough came, Randy's heart was ready. He has now danced all over the world with the ministry he founded called Dance Ad Deum (which means "Dance unto God") and is recognized internationally as one of the pioneers of modern Christian dance. Even more exciting, Randy has won many people to Christ.

> *To see spiritual breakthroughs, we have to keep asking until the answer comes; we have to keep knocking until the doors open.*

To see spiritual breakthroughs, we have to keep asking until the answer comes; we have to keep knocking until the doors open. Laboring to bring forth revival, whether personal or corporate, is no easy process. We cannot make God move, but the condition of our hearts tells Him if we are ready for Him to move. We must travail and persevere like a woman during an intense labor before birthing a baby. Too often, we want God to move His hand for revival, but if we would touch His heart, He would naturally move His hand.

Exemplifying tenacity and perseverance, the apostle Paul wrote, *"I press toward the goal for the prize of the upward call of God in Christ Jesus"* (Philippians 3:14). Notice that there is a process of pressing in, enduring to run the race to completion. Our bodies get fatigued; our minds battle thoughts like, *I can't do it. It's too hard. It's too long. There's no way I can make it.* But the Spirit says, "You *can* do it. Because of what Christ has already done, you can go the distance." Jesus has already run the race, and He is the joy set before us.

How do we persevere when our minds battle the thought that we are doomed to fail? We push forward anyway. We call on a fellow Christian and ask for prayer. We saturate our minds in the Word because we are promised that *"[God] will keep him in perfect peace, whose mind is stayed on You"* (Isaiah 26:3). We renew our minds by washing them in the water of the Word. We hold on to Him at all cost.

Our minds are the gateway to our hearts. If we give our minds to the things of this world, the world will eventually have our hearts as well. If we focus on the Lord, then He remains in the center of our minds and hearts. We must commit ourselves to persist until we have finished the race in righteousness, bringing honor to Him.

THE PRICE OF REVIVAL

Storms are certain to come; how we weather them is determined by the focus of our hearts. May the Lord be able to say of us, as He did of the church in biblical Philadelphia, *"I know your works. See, I have set before you an open door, and no one can shut it; for you have a little strength, have kept My word, and have not denied My name"* (Revelvation 3:8). The Lord is giving us open doors for the gospel. Though we may feel we have but a little strength, we need to keep running through those doors. We need to press in and pray for more changed lives and more souls to come to Christ.

We may think we have little to offer, but whatever we offer back to the Lord in purity of heart will be sufficient for what He asks us to do. We can choose to press in or we can faint along the way. God is strengthening you and me right now to press in just a little more and a little longer. If we submit to the Lord and ask Him to build His character in us, then victory is on the way.

Are we willing to pay the price for revival? Do things in our lives and the attitudes of our hearts hinder a move of God? Past revivals always began with a deep hunger for intimacy with God. From that place of intimacy comes repentance, consecration, and holiness.

Let's keep our focus on Jesus, on worshipping Him. Even though we sometimes see spectacular manifestations of His Spirit, the greatest miracles are revealed in changed lives.

9

WATER THE CAMELS

Jesus came and spoke to them, saying, "All authority has been given to Me in heaven and on earth. Go therefore and make disciples of all the nations, baptizing them in the name of the Father and of the Son and of the Holy Spirit, teaching them to observe all things that I have commanded you; and lo, I am with you always, even to the end of the age." Amen.
—Matthew 28:18–20

Years ago, near Christmastime, I was driving to a Luv Ya Houston men's meeting hosted by E. Z. Jones. Near the on-ramp of the freeway, there was a man holding a sign that read, "Corpus Christi." He had a suitcase with him. I was running late that day; unwilling to make myself even later, I started to pass him…when I felt a tug to stop. I called out to him, "Have you eaten lunch?" When he said no, I invited him to come with me and tell me what was going on with him. I learned that he was a computer programmer who had lost his job in Michigan. There was a possible job opportunity for him in Corpus Christi.

I carried his suitcase into the restaurant and into the lunch meeting. When all the businessmen who had passed him by on their way to lunch saw him, conviction fell. As a result, the compassion of God touched everyone there and E. Z. Jones felt led to take up an offering for this man.

After the lunch, I took him into my apartment for a short period of time to get him through Christmas. During that time, he became a Christian. After a few weeks, he felt led to return to Michigan, where I heard later that he became involved in a church and also got back into business.

Among those who attended that Luv Ya Houston meeting was a man in the oil business. He had been invited numerous times before, but this was the first time he had attended. Years later, he was on television and told the story of what caused him to become a Christian. The final event that brought him to the Lord was seeing a man carrying a suitcase into a restaurant, another man following him, and an offering taken up to help the stranger. That day, he saw the love of Christians and the compassion of Jesus poured out through a group of businessmen and he was propelled toward Christ.

PREPARING OUR HEARTS

People are crying out to God for revival in their own lives and for their families, their cities, and their nation. Yet this only comes with a price. God is looking for a people, a bride, with a prepared heart into which He can deposit His rich authority. The bride who will usher this generation into a relationship with the Lord must be willing to serve and to sacrifice.

The late revivalist Leonard Ravenhill once reminded my staff, "When a sacrifice is placed on the altar, the fire does not consume the altar but the sacrifice on the altar." We are that sacrifice placed on God's altar as we daily offer ourselves to Him and make ourselves available for His purposes.

Hearts that are prepared to serve and sacrifice are also willing to receive the needy people He brings our way. Some have been battered by the consequences of sin, and they may not look like the kind of people we want to hang out with. Yet if we are willing to serve them for the Lord's sake, God promises to give us power and authority to be His witnesses.

If we are willing to serve others for the Lord's sake, God promises to give us power and authority to be His witnesses.

More and more frequently, Christians are gathering in humility and asking, "God, what is Your will for the body of Christ in our city?" Together, we are becoming a corporate, anointed people who say, "God, not our will, but Your will be done." We are becoming servants who make sacrifices for souls as we serve, individually and as a body of believers, this generation of people who so desperately need the Lord.

TAMING THE TENSIONS

One of the gaps in our society is generational. Often, we have allowed that gap to hinder us from reaching out to young people. Generation gaps have caused seemingly impenetrable walls of misunderstanding between parent and child. The mistrust is even more evident among youth from broken homes.

Gang violence rises when youth turn to gangs as substitute families. Gangs provide an identity and a group—a place to belong. Are we, the body of Christ, sharing Christ's love in a way that reflects a sense of family that would draw such teens in? As violence escalates and spreads from our inner cities to suburbia and even into small town environments, our ministry of reconciliation means that we are the true peacemakers in a troubled world.

When I approached my second decade of ministry, I wondered if young people would still relate to what I shared with them. Yet the Lord continued and still continues to lead our team to the young. Some people in our ministry can identify with them; others come from quite different backgrounds. Regardless, when we reach out to young people with the love of Christ, they embrace it.

One day, Bob, one of our workers, joined me for a time of ministry at a home for troubled teens. Bob noticed how hardened and angry many of the teens were and asked them why. One young man replied, "Don't you know? We're Generation X. Our parents didn't care. We're not supposed to care."

The kids initially didn't want to talk with us because of their feelings of bitterness. They weren't angry with us; they were responding to their own hurting hearts. Eventually, the ice was broken, and we began to relate to them at their point of need. I said, "You know, some people really don't care, but there's Somebody who *does* care. He cares so much that He gave His own life for you." As uncomfortable as it might be to reach out to angry young people, we take the first step, and God takes it from there.

> *As uncomfortable as it might be to reach out to angry young people, we take the first step, and God takes it from there.*

ON THE CUTTING EDGE

Society defines each generation of young people by various names, but I like to refer to them as "Gen-Edgers"—young people living on the edge of eternity. As we sow our time and our wisdom into the younger generation and they get saved, they move to the cutting edge for Christ. Like Joshua and Caleb, they see things differently from others who spy out the promised land. (See Numbers 14:6–9.) We must dedicate ourselves to releasing these young people to their destiny, for we desperately need their vision to lead us into the revival God has for us. Without their youthful vision, we will all perish in the wilderness of endless wandering.

This generation is radical and unashamed of the gospel. As I watch our young people working in the harvest or singing passionately in worship, I can't help but say to myself, *There's my girl! That's my boy!* There is no greater joy in life than having spiritual sons and daughters whom the Lord has redeemed.

Many of our youth, however, are wandering aimlessly and without hope. A derogatory name marked Generation X, but God saw a generation of excellence. As you and I fulfill our calling to serve them, the younger generations will fulfill their God-given potential and do mighty exploits for the gospel.

As you and I fulfill our calling to serve them, the younger generations will fulfill their God-given potential and do mighty exploits for the gospel.

Hundreds of years before Christ's birth, the prophet Malachi spoke of these days in which we live: *"Behold, I will send you Elijah the prophet before the coming of the great and dreadful day of the* LORD. *And he will turn the hearts of the fathers to the children, and the hearts of the children to their fathers"* (Malachi 4:5–6). God wants to use you and me to reach this fatherless, orphaned generation.

Many on-fire Christian youth are ministering to others, and God is also using fathers in the faith and spiritual mothers to reach young hearts. With so many growing up without a dad, it is beautiful to see men of God embrace these hard-to-reach young people.

Take, for example, a pastor from southwest Houston who linked up with Somebody Cares Houston and became involved in the adopt-a-gang prayer coverage. The church adopted several gangs in the Alief area to pray for them. Then they moved from intercession to intervention, and the youth responded. What started as a youth-oriented Friday evening service with about twenty attending grew to a Saturday evening church service comprised of 250 to 300 young people of various racial and cultural backgrounds, including many kids from gangs. They began reaching out to the families, and lives were changed. It all started with a burden to pray for young people.

Bud Lenz, a former staff member who's now a missionary in Peru, and Richard Hinojosa, who worked at the citywide baptism at the water park, were part of an initial group of youth ministers who developed an arm of Somebody Cares known as Youth Guidance Consultants (YGC). YGC provided training to volunteers, teachers, school officials, and community service workers who worked with at-risk youth and gang members. The hands-on work with the youth started as Richard reached out to young people in a local public school. He simply hung out with the kids during lunchtime and built relationships with them, their teachers, and principals.

Eventually, with Richard's help, we developed a six-hour training seminar to identify and intervene in cases of at-risk youth behavior, which helped teachers and administrators deal with real-life questions, such as how to break up a fight. Working together with Bud, Ernie Lopez, and the late Max Torres, we then developed a handbook that was so effective, it has been used by school districts and the Houston mayor's Anti-Gang Task Force. The Houston police department's outreach division adopted it as a training manual. Those of our group who completed it received I.D. badges provided by the police department to go work in schools.

Richard also developed the "Hero" curriculum, a biblically based character-development curriculum that was used in secular schools. Community leaders took notice of the program's effectiveness and wanted to know more.

RESTORING HEARTS IN A FATHERLESS SOCIETY

Today God is calling the church to go forth in the spirit of an Elijah or a John the Baptist to prepare this generation for His coming. As preparation is made for the Lord's return, many in this generation will have hearts turned back not only to their earthly fathers but also to the heavenly Father.

A few years ago, a fourteen-year-old boy on the streets told us, "Mom had to choose between me and her boyfriend—and I lost." Over the years, we have worked with many runaways and teen prostitutes. One of these young women said she was left at a motel to fend for herself at the age of eight! To reach this generation of young people, we need to understand this breakdown of the parental role. I am particularly sensitive to this problem, for I often felt unsettled following my own parents' divorce when I was a young boy.

Our cities are filled with young people who are virtual orphans—victims of an increasingly fatherless society.

Our cities are filled with young people who are virtual orphans—victims of an increasingly fatherless society. Can you feel the pain and hopelessness of this fatherless generation? Do you see why they feel destined for destruction instead of success? As one kid on the street told me, "There are only two ways off the streets—the penitentiary or the grave." Fortunately, Jesus offers a real alternative.

PASSING THE BATON TO A RADICAL GENERATION

"Generation Jesus" in Houston had a great impact on the emerging generation. They were a devoted group of young people ranging in age from teens to late twenties. Many of them lived radical lives of sin but turned their hearts toward Christ. They were led by E. Z. Jones, the man who gave me an apartment to live in during the mid-1980s.

E. Z. and Lena Jones could have chosen to be uninvolved with young people by using the excuse that they're from another era. They could have cast judgmental stares at the green-haired, body-pierced young people around them. Instead, they pastored to this on-fire group of young people. Teens often knocked on their door at one or two o'clock in the morning, but E. Z. and Lena would rather be awakened in the middle of the night than identify their young people in the morgue or officiate at their funerals. Former addicts and gang leaders were so hungry for God that when it was time for the weekly Generation Jesus services to end, they didn't want to leave. These teens grew quickly as disciples of the Lord. As E. Z. said of them, "They don't ask each other, 'What church do you go to?' They just love each other, pray with each other, and praise God together."

One day, E. Z. called me following a powerful night of ministry with Generation Jesus. He said, "I looked around the room, reflected on what the Lord was doing, and suddenly realized this is the clubhouse of the same apartment complex where you had a move of God in the 1980s! I looked out the clubhouse window and saw the apartment we rented for you, Doug."

E. Z. reminisced about the time he walked into my apartment and saw a bunch of young people sleeping on the floor. In the same clubhouse where Generation Jesus first held its meetings, I held Bible studies with those young people. E. Z. and Lena asked if I would come one evening and minister to Generation Jesus, pray for the young people, and symbolically pass the baton. My heart rejoiced that from a seed planted years ago, a new breed of radical youth has arisen to reach their generation for Christ.

While some may have given up hope for the coming generation, God certainly has not. Many young people are finding direction and purpose for their lives. There is a rising hunger among the youth. God is giving them a mantle of John the Baptist. They have a prophetic mantle to stand and declare, "Prepare ye the way of the Lord" to their generation.

Today many young people are being reached and are ministering to others with fervor and zeal. We have a responsibility to encourage them and share with them any wisdom we may have gleaned during our years in ministry.

IN SEARCH OF THE BRIDE

Abraham once sent out a servant in search of a bride for his son, Isaac. (See Genesis 24.) Likewise, our heavenly Father is sending out His Holy Spirit to search for a bride for His Son, Jesus. Throughout Scripture, we find types and shadows, people and events that represent a message the Lord is sharing with us today. In this Genesis passage, Abraham represents a type of the heavenly Father, and his servant represents a type of the Holy Spirit. Isaac is a type of Jesus, and the bride represents the church.

Throughout Scripture, we find types and shadows, people and events that represent a message the Lord is sharing with us today.

When Abraham sent out his servant, he gave him ten camels, which carried the basic necessities for traveling through the desert and bore gifts to bestow upon the bride. Today the heavenly Father has sent out His Holy Spirit in search of a bride prepared to serve Him and people in need. As we, the church, become that bride for Jesus, the heavenly Father bestows upon us His provision and His gifts.

The key trait that Abraham's servant sought in a bride for Isaac was that she be willing to serve her master and those in need. Abraham's servant stopped at the town well and found such a woman. She gave him a drink of water and was also willing to water his ten thirsty camels, which were also dirty, hungry, and stinky.

I have heard it said that one camel completing that desert journey could drink approximately forty gallons of water. Ten camels would then need 400 gallons of water, and this young woman drew it all from the well! As she served those camels, she did not realize that they bore gifts for her. She simply looked for the opportunity to serve. In the same way, the heavenly Father is looking for a bride for His Son—a bride who is willing to serve Him and those thirsty camels.

Many of us are like those dirty, stinky camels coming out of the wilderness. We have pasts filled with addictive behaviors, immoral lifestyles, and futile searches to satisfy our longing souls. But God has fed us and cleaned us up.

This current generation has the same needs. They are trying countless ways to cover up their fears, insecurities, and pain. God wants to transform them into a John the Baptist generation, preparing the way of the Lord. As their lives are changed through Christ, this generation of young people will be true witnesses who rescue others.

SERVING AND SAVING THIS GENERATION

The prophet Joel recorded:

It shall come to pass afterward that I will pour out My Spirit on all flesh; your sons and your daughters shall prophesy, your old men shall dream dreams, your young men shall see visions. And also on My menservants and on My maidservants I will pour out My Spirit in those days. (Joel 2:28–29)

Genuine prophets and prophetesses are those who will live a radical life for God and boldly proclaim His truth and mercy to a generation coming out of the desert. Today's young people are keenly aware of where they have been and the heartache they have experienced. As they come to know the living God, they become radical for Him. They are not ashamed of the gospel of Christ, for they have experienced it as the power of God for salvation. (See Romans 1:16.) Because they have wandered in the wilderness of life, today's young people are destined to become a prophetic generation, proclaiming the word of the Lord and preparing the way for His coming.

God loves the coming generation and wants to set them free. He is giving you and me the opportunity and the privilege to boldly share the gospel with them. But are we willing to work with those whom we might consider to be unlovely? Will we go the extra mile with them? God is challenging us to get out of our comfort zone and reach out to others with a servant's heart and sacrificial love.

10

REVIVAL BY CHOICE OR BY JUDGMENT?

Now it shall come to pass in the latter days that the mountain of the LORD's house shall be established on the top of the mountains, and shall be exalted above the hills; and all nations shall flow to it. Many people shall come and say, "Come, and let us go up to the mountain of the LORD, to the house of the God of Jacob; He will teach us His ways, and we shall walk in His paths." For out of Zion shall go forth the law, and the word of the LORD from Jerusalem. He shall judge between the nations, and rebuke many people; they shall beat their swords into plowshares, and their spears into

> *pruning hooks; nation shall not lift up sword against nation,*
> *neither shall they learn war anymore."*
> —Isaiah 2:2–4 (see also Micah 4:1–3)

Some years ago, God moved my heart to start a regular Sunday service for those saved through our ministry. For years, I resisted the idea, even when those same people told me they felt awkward going immediately to mainline churches and needed a transition place to gather. I believed I was called to build the body of Christ in the city, to identify and encourage the ministries already established rather than start a local church myself. But when pastors started urging me as well, I prayed earnestly, then rented a hotel room as a meeting place.

First, we called the new church Edge City; then we changed the name to Turning Point Christian Center. We opened the membership to those who came to Jesus through our ministry and those who came with a letter of release and blessing from their local pastor. If a Christian wanted to join us, we told the person that he or she could come as a missionary under the auspices of a local church and return to that local church when the mission was accomplished.

I disbanded the church once, telling the members that their transition period was over and they needed to get attached to local churches. Two months later, I reopened the doors and started again, and we immediately grew with new converts and those who had not been able to become involved elsewhere.

The church continued to meet for a few years and the new converts made their transitions. Recognizing the importance of investing in our city, we redirected to citywide corporate services.

Our goal is to help co-pastor the city and do our part to reach out to the community in tangible ways.

We have to be willing to do whatever God asks in order to see more of His purposes come to pass in our cities. In my heart, I know there is more—more unity to be nurtured, more perseverance needed, more brokenness to heal, and more souls to be added. I teach our converts that true revival will first be a revival of holiness and consecration.

> *In my heart, I know there is more—*
> *more unity to be nurtured, more perseverance*
> *needed, more brokenness to heal,*
> *and more souls to be added.*

I often pray, "Lord, how are You going to set Your church ablaze with a hunger for Your holiness?" We say we want revival and we want the church to work together to be part of a harvest, yet at times, our actions speak a contrary message. What will it take to bring a lasting revival to our land?

There is nothing wrong with going to services and having the Lord minister to us in a way that makes us feel good, but there is more to revival than that. In fact, there are times when our need is not for something to make us feel good. Before there can be genuine times of refreshing, there must be times of repentance.

Have we been broken before the Lord over our own sin, including sins of omission? Our sin doesn't have to be something we've done; sometimes, it is something we have left undone. We must ask ourselves whether we are truly concerned for the welfare of others. A move of God that does not lead to changed lives and lost souls coming to Christ falls short of being a true revival. A genuine revival is not a matter of hoopla or emotion or even spiritual refreshing; it is a matter of transforming individuals and then entire communities.

AT A CROSSROADS

A few years ago on a radio program, I was asked if I thought God was going to bring judgment or revival to America. I paused for a moment and replied, "Both." God is going to bring revival to His people, and it will either come by choice or by judgment. We are at a crossroads as a nation and as the church. The choices we make today will determine our future.

The late Dr. Richard Halverson, chaplain of the U.S. Senate from 1981 to 1994 and author of several books, succinctly summed up the history of the church: "Christianity started in Palestine as a relationship with a person—Jesus. It went to Greece and became a philosophy, went to Rome and became an institution, and went to Europe and became a culture. Then it came to America and became an enterprise."

> *The Lord will not force us to consecrate our lives, but He can surely put pressure on us to seek Him.*

The Lord will not force us to consecrate our lives, but He can surely put pressure on us to seek Him. He will do whatever it takes to get our attention. We will either surrender all to Him and birth revival or, through our disobedience, He will allow judgment to come. We will go to our knees to seek Him either by choice or by judgment.

If we do not rise up and fulfill our calling to prepare people for His coming, God will have to shake us. Therefore, we must lay aside anything that hinders us, individually or corporately. We cannot give in to fears and insecurities or engage in blame. This is not a time to play games with God. His Word states that everything that can be shaken will be shaken until only that which cannot be shaken remains. (See Hebrews 12:26–27.)

Although it is never God's desire to bring destruction, He wants our total devotion. He desires to possess the thrones of our hearts. When the Lord breathes His life in us and through us, nothing can stop His impact on our lives and communities. How will we withstand the wind and the shaking? It all depends on the condition of our hearts.

HANG ON!

Three things will take place during shaking. For one, those who have left their first-love relationship with the Lord will be shaken until they return to God's stern but merciful, loving hand.

Obstacles in the way of the gospel will also be removed, such as people or ministries that are cosmetic only. Jesus told a parable about a landowner who came seeking fruit on his fig tree but found none. From a distance, the fig tree probably had plenty of leaves and must have appeared capable of bearing figs. But as the owner approached, he was disappointed that there were no figs. (See Luke 13:6–9.) If those who produce only leaves but no fruit refuse to repent, God will replace them with those who are preaching the pure gospel and bearing genuine fruit.

During the shaking, God will also restore those who feel forsaken—those who have served the Lord with sincerity and integrity, fighting the good fight and loving the sheep, yet have become *weary while doing good* (Galatians 6:9). Those who have been faithful through all the trials and have kept their stand for God's righteousness will receive blessings in order to perpetuate the gospel and experience a great outpouring of God's Spirit.

Beyond the shaking is the promise and the hope set before us. We must pray for our ministers and leaders as they undergo relentless attacks during shaking. We must pray for the body of Christ as well. This is not a day to give up on the church, or on yourself, and certainly not on the Lord. Instead, it is a day for us to get on our knees and seek the Lord for His grace.

He is raising up people who want to see a true outpouring of the Holy Spirit. It will not be limited to any one crusade or meeting, but the Holy Spirit will move through individuals, ministries, and churches that are prepared. God is looking for a people who are hungry for His character and a deeper relationship with Him—a people who pursue holiness over happiness. He will shake anything in our lives that distracts us from Him, so we must seek Him with all our hearts and press in to Him as never before.

> *God is looking for a people who are hungry for His character and a deeper relationship with Him—a people who pursue holiness over happiness.*

THE LATTER RAIN IS STARTING

Bob Ferguson, wearing one of his ever-present baseball caps, walked alone into one of our Friday night Bible studies, looking like a stereotypical Houston redneck and not at all like the recovering heroin addict he really was. Bob's father had died, leaving him feeling empty inside. When his AA sponsor died as well, Bob's heart quit feeling anything except a steady ache.

When people from AA dropped out of the group occasionally to attend church, Bob would become angry. "They think they're too good for us," he reasoned. Finally, when another friend became a Christian, Bob asked, "What are you doing?"

"Man, I'm getting to know Jesus!" the friend said.

Bob had grown up in a traditional church and believed in the one true God, but he had never learned about Jesus. The concept intrigued him. One night, Bob gave his life to the Lord while I was teaching an eight-week series on "The Work of the Cross." He came forward, saying, "God is real! God is real!" and started weeping.

"Man, You're slick," Bob told God as he confessed Christ as His Lord. Suddenly, he knew that Jesus was the way to the Father and that he was no longer alone. He realized that no matter who came or went on earth, he would never be fatherless again.

Each week, Bob continued to weep as he listened with a grateful heart. He knew he was finally hearing unvarnished, absolute truth. A month later, he asked about baptism, and we baptized him that night in the hot tub at the Holiday Inn.

Bob was exuberant in his Christian witness. I had been teaching on the spirit of adoption that we receive through Christ, and Bob found everyone he could to adopt. He took literally the idea that he was now a minister of reconciliation, regardless of the lack of certificates hanging on his wall. Weeks later, on a campout with a friend, Bob took out his Bible for morning devotions.

"You going thumping?" his friend chided, thinking Bob was going to start preaching.

"I'm having my morning prayer," Bob replied. "Want to be included?"

Scriptures popped into Bob's mind and he shared them with his friend, and the man repented and received Christ. Then the friend asked Bob to baptize him right there in the lake. Bob didn't know what to do except just to do it, so he baptized his friend in the name of the Father, the Son, and the Holy Spirit.

"I'm 99.5 percent certain that you're okay, but you'd better get baptized again when we get back, just in case," Bob told the man. Immediately, he remembered that Jesus had called him to minister and he said, "I take it back. You're 100 percent legal. You're baptized, man!"

LETTING OUR LIGHT SHINE

Isaiah wrote, *"Arise, shine; for your light has come!"* (Isaiah 60:1). Though we know the light of the Lord is going to get brighter, the following verse reads, *"Darkness shall cover the earth."* As God's light gets brighter, darkness will get darker, yet God will pour out great wonders:

> *I will show wonders in the heavens and in the earth: blood and fire and pillars of smoke. The sun shall be turned into darkness, and the moon into blood, before the coming of the great and awesome day of the LORD.*   (Joel 2:30–31)

As God pours out His Spirit, we are also going to see an onslaught of the enemy. We must prepare, let go of old ways, and become lovers of truth, so we will not be deceived by the schemes and temptations of the evil one.

> *We must prepare, let go of old ways, and become lovers of truth, so we will not be deceived by the schemes and temptations of the evil one.*

Scripture warns of false prophets in the last days and predicts that many people will reject the truth because they want their ears tickled—they want to hear only what makes them feel good. No matter how uncomfortable the truth makes us feel, we must love it more than life itself, for it is the truth that sets us free. (See John 8:32.)

We also need to be planted in the household of faith when the dark gets darker. We are instructed in Scripture not to forsake the fellowship of the saints, and this will be all the more crucial in the days preceding the return of Christ. (See Hebrews 10:25.) We must care for one another, helping our brothers and sisters in their maturing process as believers. Likewise, we must prepare to take in those who will find shelter under the wings of God.

The prophet Joel said, *"It shall come to pass that whoever calls on the name of the LORD shall be saved"* (Joel 2:32). Peter quotes this verse (see Acts 2:21), as does Paul (see Romans 10:13). Joel continues, *"For in Mount Zion and in Jerusalem there shall be deliverance."* Deliverance can only come as an outcome of the salvation of the Lord. God wants to bring salvation, healing, and deliverance to our lives and to the lives of those He will redeem during this great outpouring.

We cannot separate the terms *salvation* and *deliverance*, for with salvation comes deliverance. That is the hope for our lives and for the multitudes still in the valley of decision. The Lord is calling people to Himself.

Bob Ferguson is a great example of this kind of outpouring. His love for God is so exuberant, so irrepressible, that dozens and perhaps hundreds of people by now have followed him into salvation. He's just a regular guy, a former heroin junkie, who loves and exudes truth wherever he goes.

BETWEEN THE PORCH AND THE ALTAR

We love to hear about revival happening to others, but we also long to see a mighty outpouring of God's Spirit in our own lives, as on the day of Pentecost. Scripture says, *"Let the priests, who minister to the LORD, weep between the porch and the altar"* (Joel 2:17). Who are the priests referred to here? That's us—because we are *"a royal priesthood, a holy nation"* (1 Peter 2:9). We must repent and weep between the porch and the altar. We must stand between the living and the dead and stop the plague of sin. (See Numbers 16:48.) How is the plague stopped? By personal repentance and revival, which brings personal refreshing. At that place of brokenness in *our* lives, the plague of sin will be stopped in *their* lives.

Any of us who are leaders, or want to be considered as such, must weep between the porch and the altar. The apostle Paul said, *"Imitate me, just as I also imitate Christ"* (1 Corinthians 11:1). We must set an example that Jesus would want the sheep to follow.

> *We must repent and weep between the porch and the altar. We must stand between the living and the dead and stop the plague of sin.*

Joel issued a charge to ministers to cry out to the Lord, saying, *"Spare Your people, O Lord, and do not give Your heritage to reproach, that the nations should rule over them. Why should they say among the peoples, 'Where is their God?'"* (Joel 2:17).

The world is desperate to see that what Christians have is the real deal. As tragedies are reported on the nightly news all over the world, people are awaiting the church's response. Faced with fires, riots, murders, economic crashes, and more, people wonder, *Where is God?* We must show them by manifesting His glory and power in the midst of tragedy.

I believe we are living on borrowed time. Those who are producing fruit will be pruned so they will produce even more or better fruit. Those who are not producing fruit will be moved aside to make room for those who will. God will show us both His goodness and His severity. (See Romans 11:22.) It begins with us. In other words, those outside the church must see the love and power of God in action through living, breathing temples of the Holy Spirit. *That's you and me. Our preaching will have more impact when our message is something we actually live.* When we go forth as witnesses for Christ, walking in the love of God, then God will begin to manifest His presence, and signs, wonders, and miracles will follow.

MAKING WAY FOR THE NEW

The Lord said, through the prophet Joel, *"Behold, I will send you grain and new wine and oil"* (Joel 2:19). A grain has to die so that new grain can spring up. (See John 12:24.) For our vats to be full of new wine and oil, the old has to be emptied out. We have to let go of the old nature, the old ways, to have the new things God has in store for us. We must let go even of the good so we can have that which is better.

When God begins to pour out His Spirit upon us, often He begins to shake up our lives so that the things that can be shaken fall down and the things that cannot be shaken are left standing. God begins to fill us with a new perception of things, a new way of thinking, a new attitude, and a new character.

When that process is complete, He is able to pour out His Spirit because He can trust us to be vessels He can fill with His power.

God took the children of Israel out of Egypt, but before they could enter the promised land, He had to *take Egypt out of them.* When we go through the wilderness experiences of life, God deals with the sins of Egypt that still reside in our hearts.

> *When we seek God's face and cry out to Him for personal revival, He will begin to reveal our false beliefs, areas of disobedience, and bad attitudes.*

When we seek God's face and cry out to Him for personal revival, He will begin to reveal our false beliefs, areas of disobedience, and bad attitudes. He removes old ways and teaches us His ways. He uproots the remnants of the old nature and shows us the things that need to die. As we trust Him to do this work, transformation begins. We become ready for the new grain, the new wine, and the new oil.

God has been transforming us into His image since the day we accepted Christ. He wants the old nature crucified so that we can fulfill His purposes upon the earth. Paul encourages us, *"Therefore, if anyone is in Christ, he is a new creation; old things have passed away; behold, all things have become new"* (2 Corinthians 5:17). When we come to the cross of Christ, we come to a place of death—death to self. Our old nature is buried so we can rise up in newness to an abundant life in Christ. But to receive the newness God desires for us, we have to die to the past.

Old wheat has to die; old wineskins have to go. Old oil must be poured out so He can bless us with new oil. *"Behold, all things have become new"* is God's desire. We cannot bypass the death process. The apostle Paul said, *"Therefore put to death your members which are on the earth: fornication, uncleanness, passion, evil desire, and covetousness, which is idolatry"* (Colossians 3:5). Why should we put such things to death? Because holding on to them means denying Christ's lordship in those areas of our lives.

Paul goes on to warn, *"The wrath of God is coming upon the sons of disobedience"* (verse 6). Let's not be found to be disobedient children, even though we might have been in the past. And let us not merely settle for external or cosmetic righteousness, for Paul continues, *"But now you yourselves are to put off all these: anger, wrath, malice, blasphemy, filthy language out of your mouth"* (Colossians 3:8). After dealing with overt sins in the previous verses, Paul emphasizes that God also wants to deal with anger and other matters of the heart.

ALL THINGS BECOME NEW

In the death and renewal process, first the outward sins are cleansed and then He begins to deal with us about matters of the heart—our thoughts, attitudes, and words. We are in a spiritual battle, but it is not only against satanic principalities and powers. The battle begins in our minds:

For though we walk in the flesh, we do not war according to the flesh. For the weapons of our warfare are not carnal but mighty in God for pulling down strongholds, casting down arguments and every high thing that exalts itself against the knowledge of God, bringing every thought into captivity to the obedience of Christ, and being ready to punish all disobedience when your obedience is fulfilled. (2 Corinthians 10:3–6)

God wants to take us to an intimate place of relationship with Him.
He wants to show us great and awesome things and use us to reach our generation.

God wants to take us to an intimate place of relationship with Him. He wants to show us His manifest presence and glory. He wants to show us great and awesome things and use us to reach our generation. Will we become vessels into which He can pour His Spirit? Will we be vessels of honor into which He can deposit His power for His purpose?

JESUS DID IT

Almost everyone from our new converts' congregation is involved in some form of ministry somewhere in our city. Bob Ferguson, the least likely to have become a true minister, is ablaze with the fire of God's revival.

Bob's foul language stopped immediately after his salvation. His temper came under control. God delivered Him from pornography and other vices. As a wrecker driver, he would occasionally drop by our office in the middle of the day just to say, "I need prayer." Someone would pray with him, then he'd go on his way. After smoking three packs of cigarettes a day for twenty-three years, Bob started praying about that habit. A year after his conversion, he asked me to anoint him with oil because he believed he was near a breakthrough. Then he quit smoking. Overnight.

That gave Bob the idea that Jesus could intervene with habits his friends were trying to kick in the AA groups. When they asked how he quit, Bob would just say, "Jesus did it." He was a walking miracle who had kicked heroin, methadone, and nicotine. He started bringing Jesus into the twelve-step group. After Houston Prayer Mountain, he started his own group called Jesus in the Steps. This program is not a twelve-step program but a fourteen-step program with Jesus as the first and last steps, the Alpha and the Omega, the beginning and the end. Today many such groups are thriving in Houston. People are learning the truth of who Jesus is.

God wants us to die to our flesh and embrace truth, loving it even more than life itself, because He has more for us. He wants to move through us by His Spirit and bring multitudes into His kingdom. He is preparing hearts now for an outpouring of His Spirit. While some of us will experience a great outpouring of grace and blessing like Bob did, others will experience judgment to deal with compromise and complacency. If our society is going to change, the change must begin with us.

11

OUR DATE WITH DESTINY

Therefore let us not sleep, as others do,
but let us watch and be sober.
—1 Thessalonians 5:6

Brenda didn't know a soul when she went. All she knew as a single mom was that a free meal for her four children was too good to pass up, even if it came with some strings attached. Despite her misgivings about using the gasoline, Brenda loaded her children into the old Buick and drove to the *Supper Bowl* in Tampa, Florida, the weekend before the NFL's big game. What she received was so much more than a free meal.

Professional athletes encouraged Brenda's children to do well in school and told them it didn't cost a penny to gain self-discipline and learn diligence. Ministers told stories of people who had come up from neighborhoods like hers and built tremendous lives for themselves based on their faith in God. Some workers at the event took an interest in Brenda and told her their church had an outreach for single mothers. For the first time in four years, Brenda felt something so unusual that, at first, she couldn't figure out what it was. Hope was birthed in her heart that day.

Multiply Brenda's story hundreds of times and you understand the impact Somebody Cares Tampa Bay is making on their community by coordinating with sports teams and Christian athletes. They have evangelized their city with stadium events and created feeding programs in conjunction with the local Rays sports team. They have linked arms with the Book of Hope campaign, helped to facilitate large evangelistic concerts, and coordinated with Operation Blessing to conduct school assemblies and massive feedings.

In addition, they hold an annual Compassion Banquet, where they invite the media to help them recognize and appreciate the work of dozens of frontline ministries. I was at the kick-off meeting for Somebody Cares Tampa Bay when a hundred pastors signed a covenant of unity. Somebody Cares Tampa Bay director Dan Bernard is ensuring that the Brendas of his community receive help to raise their children as productive citizens and have the opportunity to receive Christ as Savior and Lord.

WHO IS OUR NEIGHBOR?

Fruitful Christians seize opportunities to be Jesus's witnesses. Fruitless Christians squander opportunities. Although we may be believers, failure to take action leaves us powerless and fruitless. True Christianity on the inside, with its corresponding actions, is marked by the power of God. It brings change, ushers in revival, and awakens the society around it.

> *True Christianity on the inside, with its corresponding actions, is marked by the power of God.*

A *"certain lawyer"* asked Jesus what he must do to inherit eternal life. Since the man knew the Old Testament Scriptures well, Jesus asked him what they said. The man responded, *"'You shall love the LORD your God with all your heart, with all your soul, with all your strength, and with all your mind,' and 'your neighbor as yourself'"* (Luke 10:27). Jesus told the lawyer that his answer was correct and if he would do this, he would live.

The lawyer had all the right words, but Jesus was probing his heart to see if his actions would speak the same message. *We can have the right answer without having a right heart.*

Jesus demonstrated that the lawyer was intent only on justifying himself. Instead of being humbled by the requirements of God's law, the man tried to find an escape clause by asking, *"Who is my neighbor?"* (verse 29).

Jesus wasn't about to let the lawyer wriggle out of his responsibilities. Although the man wanted to pick and choose his neighbors so he could be judged as righteous, Jesus ended the discussion with shocking news: everyone we encounter is our neighbor!

Jesus then told the story of the Good Samaritan. (See Luke 10:30–37.) A priest and a Levite passed by a man who had been beaten, robbed, and left half dead, but a Samaritan—whose people were despised by the Jews—stopped to help. According to some theologians, the priest who passed by was going to minister in the temple, an honor bestowed on him only once every few years. The priest felt that by helping the wounded man, he would miss his opportunity. Yet he failed to recognize that ministry is all about reaching people. By ignoring the man who was bleeding and dying, the priest passed up an opportunity to show love to his neighbor.

A DOER OF THE WORD

In Florida, a man's son was in a hospital, dying of leukemia. One day, while heading to the hospital, the father noticed a homeless boy on the street. The father could have responded like the priest or the Levite because he was already caring for his son. He could have justified ignoring the homeless boy by saying, "I have my own problems; I can't take care of any more."

Yet even with his own son critically ill, the man stopped. He saw a need—a little boy who was homeless, destitute, and hungry—and that became his immediate calling. He looked beyond his own circumstances and even the needs of his own child to help a homeless stranger. As a result of this man taking the time to help, the boy grew into a young man who now directs a worldwide ministry to children and the homeless.

The Good Samaritan must have had a degree of wealth because he was able to pay for the wounded man's hotel and food. Yet even if he had his own business to attend to, when he found a man bleeding and dying on the side of the road, he gladly tended to the man's wounds and took him to a place of rest and shelter. This was not goose bumps love—it was *love in action.*

At the end of the story, Jesus turned to the lawyer and said, "*Go and do likewise*" (Luke 10:37). Like the lawyer, we need to go beyond giving the right answers and the correct theological formulations. We must be "*doers of the word, and not hearers only*" (James 1:22).

DON'T MISS THE GREEN LIGHT

One evening, I was driving home late, exhausted and bleary-eyed, anxious to make the last turn and get into my own driveway. As I waited for the left-turn light, a carload of people drove up beside me. I looked over at them. They didn't have a green light so they didn't move. I watched them for a moment or two, and as I did, my light turned green, then yellow, then red. When I looked forward again, I had missed the green light!

The next morning, I thought about that again and realized that at one time or another, each of us misses an opportunity because we get distracted. We can only be His witnesses if we keep our eyes on Him.

At one time or another, each of us misses an opportunity because we get distracted. We can only be His witnesses if we keep our eyes on Him.

In addition to being focused on the Lord, we must be alert for opportunities to minister to those He brings across our path. *If we're looking in the right direction, we will see the light turn green and go!*

A man who responded to the altar call for salvation at Heal Our Land Houston had been in a cult most of his life. Because of a serious accident, he was disabled and incapable of working. His girlfriend supported them as a stripper. The man asked me in all sincerity, "Doug, what should we do? If she quits her job, that's our only income."

How would you respond? We called on the Lord, and the man and his girlfriend decided she would quit her job, even though they had no idea how they would make a living. We referred them to a church, which they attended that following Sunday. During the service, the man was miraculously healed of his disability and was able to go back to work.

The more we become involved in the harvest, the more we are confronted by perplexing situations. Do our words and our testimonies show the love of God? Can people trust us? Do we trust God to solve the world's problems?

The apostle Paul exhorts us to stay awake and alert, remaining watchful and sober lest the day of the Lord overtake us as a thief in the night. (See 1 Thessalonians 5:1–11.) The day of the Lord won't overtake us in total surprise if we have watched, prayed, and gone about the business of the Lord. We can't know the day or the hour of His coming, but because we're in tune with the Holy Spirit, we can recognize the changing of the seasons.

> *We can't know the day or the hour of His coming, but because we're in tune with the Holy Spirit, we can recognize the changing of the seasons.*

A couple newly out of college came to Houston and got involved with our ministry reaching out to street kids before they ended up moving to the Dallas area. After Pam read an article in *Good Housekeeping* magazine about a woman in Oregon who was writing letters and sending Christmas gifts to sick children, she tracked down the woman's phone number. After talking with her, she was moved to begin doing something similar in Texas. She contacted us and knew this idea had a natural home with Somebody Cares. That's how Precious Parcels—a ministry of prayer, letter writing, and gift sending to sick children—was born. Pam seized an opportunity and it turned into a tremendous ministry of comfort and encouragement for terminally ill children and their parents.

In its first two years, Precious Parcels mailed 1,089 letters and over a hundred Christmas and birthday gifts. It sponsored events such as the Leukemia Society of America's "Light the Night" Walk and the Dallas White Rock Marathon to benefit a children's hospital in Dallas, where much-needed surgical operations for children are provided at no charge to their families. Many people along the way donated stickers, stamps, writing materials such as postcards and envelopes, and toys to be used as birthday and Christmas gifts.

A grateful father wrote, "We can't even begin to tell you how much it means to Nicole (age 11). We tell everyone about Precious Parcels. What means the most to us is the prayers. Without them and God's help, we would never make it. All we can say is we love what you do, and thank you."

A mother wrote, "I am Vincent's (age 6) mother and I would like to say thank you for helping him look forward to each day. When I go check the mail, he asks me, 'Did I receive mail?' He can tell by the stickers on the envelopes which letters are for him. Thank you so much."

Pam remarks, "As with any ministry, there are good days and bad days. Our worst days are when we have to say goodbye to one of these little ones as they go to meet the Lord. We know God has always held them in the palm of His hand and that now they have no sickness and no pain. It is for the families that we grieve and pray. God works all things together for good."

I was on the receiving end of a similar ministry during my battle with cancer in 2015. A dear friend, Patricia Laredo, gifted us with a pillow of peace—pillows with Scripture verses written on them to bring the comfort of God's Word while we sleep. It was such a precious gift that we started making our own pillows of peace to give to people we visited in the hospital and others who were going through difficulties.

FRUITFUL OR FRUITLESS?

When we get distracted and fail to seize opportunities to minister to others and to follow closely after Jesus, we can be categorized as having one of three heart conditions depicted in Jesus's parable of the sown seeds. (See Luke 8:11–15.) One of the most prevalent attitudes is to become distracted by the cares or the riches and pleasures of life. We can interpret this as getting distracted by the frustrations, disappointments, and hurts that occur along life's way instead of maintaining an eternal perspective on life's circumstances and racing on to the finish line.

While people are hungering and thirsting for truth and for answers to life's dilemmas, we have something of substance to offer them, and we will be able to offer it if we keep our eyes on Jesus. If we allow our roots to go deep, we will not be uprooted or fall when the winds of life come or the shaking begins. To be fruitful Christians, we must abide in Christ and allow Him to tenderize our hearts to the needs around us. Let's get ready, for our greatest tests and greatest opportunities are yet to come!

> *To be fruitful Christians, we must abide in Christ and allow Him to tenderize our hearts to the needs around us.*

When we exalt Jesus and meditate on His promises, we will overcome all that opposes His will and purpose for our lives. When we hear lies such as, "You have no fight in you, and you will not be able to go another day," we can bring that thought *"into captivity to the obedience of Christ"* (2 Corinthians 10:5). During intense times, victory will only come as we fix our hearts on Jesus.

THE DEVIL WANTS OUR RIGHT EYE

The devil wants to distract us so that we will miss opportunities and not fulfill our purpose. He wants to divert our focus to the things of this world and take our hearts captive to lust, idolatry, fear, doubt, and discouragement. Satan tries to negate the authority we have in Christ by stealing the Word of God out of our hearts and robbing us of the vision God has given us. He wants to stop us from reaching souls, and he wants to destroy us in the process.

In an Old Testament account, the men of Jabesh Gilead feared a ruler named Nahash, whose name means serpent—a clear picture of the devil. (See 1 Samuel 11.) They desired to make a covenant that would mean their servitude to Nahash but would give them a peaceful coexistence. What a deception to think that we could have peaceful coexistence with the devil, who will only be satisfied with our total humiliation and destruction!

Nahash replied, *"On this condition I will make a covenant with you, that I may put out all your right eyes, and bring reproach on all Israel"* (1 Samuel 11:2).

The right eye was significant because a soldier took up his shield in his left hand and his sword in his right hand. In order to gauge the enemy's location, he would look around the shield with his right eye. Without that eye, the soldier would be crippled in his attempt to ward off and conquer the enemy.

> *By putting out our right eyes, the devil hopes to disarm us in our efforts to accomplish Jesus's Great Commission.*

The same is true in the spiritual realm today. By putting out our right eyes, the devil hopes to disarm us in our efforts to accomplish Jesus's Great Commission. If we were to allow Satan to put out our spiritual right eyes, we would be crippled in our ability to attack and destroy the devil's work in people's lives.

The men of Jabesh Gilead succumbed to the enemy's threats instead of finding encouragement in the Lord and trusting Him. The name Jabesh means *dry*. Although these men were no doubt strong warriors, they were dry in their hearts. Their relationship to the Lord was dry, so they succumbed to unbelief and discouragement. They lost all desire to fight. Even so, God intervened, and they did not lose their ability to contend with the enemy—they did not lose their right eyes.

God has intervened on our behalf through Jesus Christ. (See 2 Corinthians 10:5.) We, too, can become weary, but we do not have to give place to discouragement and compromise when we have seemingly lost our joy, hope, and vision. Scripture reminds us:

> *And they overcame* [Satan] *by the blood of the Lamb and by the word of their testimony, and they did not love their lives to the death. Therefore rejoice, O heavens, and you who dwell in them! Woe to the inhabitants of the earth and the sea! For the devil has come down to you, having great wrath, because he knows that he has a short time.*   (Revelation 12:11–12)

MAKE JESUS "THE MAN"

God wants His people to be victorious, but sometimes we don't know how. I was invited one year to be the keynote speaker for a conference hosted by Gary Ham of Operation Breaking Through in Virginia Beach, Virginia. The conference was kicked off by a citywide prayer breakfast during which Reggie White spoke. Several years earlier, the Green Bay Packers football team had signed Reggie, and many people openly predicted that he would lead the team to the Super Bowl. Upon arriving to meet his new team, Reggie told them what it would take to become world champions. He said, "There's something we need to understand.

It's not about me, it's not about you; it's about making Brett Favre 'the man.'" Reggie said they needed to protect Favre, the quarter-back, and help him be a success. In so doing, the whole team would be a success.

That principle is the key to fulfilling our mission as the church. It's not about you, and it's not about me. It's about making Jesus "the Man." In other words, it's not about your ministry or mine, your denomination or mine; it's about lifting up the name of Jesus and extending His lordship across the earth. When He is glori-fied, we as His church are successful in our calling. But when we pursue our own interests, the whole team fails.

The Green Bay Packers did become Super Bowl champs. Who got to share in the team's victory? Reggie White, Brett Favre, and everyone associated with the Packers organization—coaches, trainers, people in the front office, and those working in less visible areas of the organization.

The whole team benefits when each member becomes content with the position he has been given. When one person is discon-tent and tries to fill someone else's position, the whole team suf-fers. To become part of a winning team, everyone in the Packers organization recognized that, individually, they had to commit to something bigger than themselves.

When Reggie speaks to ministers, he often points out that they will never fulfill their destiny unless they operate as a T.E.A.M., meaning Together Everyone Achieves More. Whether in sports or in the body of Christ, this principle is crucial to realizing our full effectiveness.

THE EDGE OF ETERNITY

When we work as a team—seeing our call to become part of something bigger than ourselves—and our hearts are prepared by remaining focused on the Lord and on souls, no catastrophic national or international event will come upon us unaware. We will not be stumped by any perplexing moral dilemma. We will not lose our *right eye ability* to fight the devil, nor will we be moved from our place of relationship with the Lord and His calling.

Throughout history, in times of peace and prosperity, we as the church have tended to compromise and become divided, concerned mostly with building our own kingdoms. We have been united mostly in times of poverty and persecution—and that is when revival has most often come. God wants to get our attention *now*. He wants us to be united in our efforts *now*. I see that happening more and more.

> Combined effort unites us as people
> and causes us to care for others more deeply than
> casual awareness allows.

Combined effort unites us as people and causes us to care for others more deeply than casual awareness allows. Uniting our efforts also creates surprising connections. One young Christian cancer patient named Wendell often went to the streets with me. Bald from chemotherapy, Wendell unashamedly walked the streets to testify of Christ's love in an effort to take as many people as possible to heaven with him. Wendell eventually died from the cancer. Sometime later, as Wendell's parents worked through their grief, they were asked to give someone a ride to church. They asked the young woman how she had come to know Christ. "I was out on the streets," she replied, "and someone named Wendell and someone named Doug told me about Jesus."

In a note to me, Leonard Ravenhill once wrote, "Let others live on the raw edge or the cutting edge. You and I should live on the edge of eternity." How can we settle into complacency while multitudes upon multitudes hang in the balance of eternity? How can we be so hard of heart as to sit back on the beach of comfort and apathy while so many are still shipwrecked in the sea of despair? How can we fight one another when the world needs us to come together with one purpose—to win souls to Christ? We have been called "*for such a time as this*" (Esther 4:14), and we must not miss our date with destiny.

12

THE NET THAT WORKS

And the Spirit and the bride say, "Come!" And let him who hears say, "Come!" And let him who thirsts come. Whoever desires, let him take the water of life freely.
—Revelation 22:17

During a street interview with a fourteen-year-old many years ago, she said with an air of pride, "I'm a prostitute. That's all I know." Yet underneath that callous exterior, Brandy was a little girl crying out for love. She gave birth to and gave away at least a couple of children that we know of during the time we worked with her.

We consistently reached out to Brandy, making sure she had our Somebody Cares business card with the telephone number. We would hear from her for a while and then there were long periods with no contact. All the same, she gave us the opportunity to give her the gospel and plant seeds of love in her heart.

Regardless of where Brandy lived or what she did for a living, she knew someone cared for her, and we knew Someone besides us had His eye on her.

Thirteen years after we met Brandy, she contracted the AIDS virus. On a chilly Friday morning in April 2000, staff member Susie Wolf pulled into the parking lot of our offices. Jen, a young prostitute, was standing there waiting and crying. As Susie approached her, Jen said, "Brandy's dead."

The shock was almost too much. So often when Brandy had called, Susie and others had gone to her aid. Even though she was in and out of jail for various charges, no one ever doubted that in the end, Brandy's life would be claimed for the kingdom of God. As Susie pieced together what had happened, she learned that after Brandy's last release from jail, she had gone to an AIDS hospice. She was incoherent at the end, yet we trust the seeds of truth planted throughout the years took root and that Brandy cried out to Jesus for life.

CASTING THE NET

When we pour ourselves into the lives of people, each person has a choice to either reject or accept our help and our Jesus.

Hollywood was an older street kid who pimped out street girls for a living. We saw him often, witnessed to him, and even got him to pray the sinner's prayer. But he never came off the streets, and that's where he died of a gunshot wound to the head. Derrah, who ran with Hollywood, heard our witness, but ended up in jail for drugs.

> *When we pour ourselves into the lives of people, each person has a choice to either reject or accept our help and our Jesus.*

Shawn prostituted herself to make a living. Opey was seduced into selling his body for food because he was starving to death. He was hooked on heavy metal music and needed deliverance. Michael bit through his tongue in a car accident and couldn't speak very well because he was constantly drooling. Although he was a nice kid, he was perceived as crazy because of his appearance, so he lived the part. Icepick was a crackhead and pimp who came off the streets...but only for a time.

Kevin went to live with a minister in another state after he broke out of the New Age movement. He was delivered of his music addiction when he took the guitar a warlock had given to him and broke it. Diana was a lesbian who saw gay men being saved and followed their path to the altar, which radically changed and freed her. One night after working at a strip club, Regina found a Somebody Cares tract left on her car and decided maybe there was hope for her. She called the number and committed her life to Christ.

Fear of others' rejection is no reason to allow hell to claim their lives. We must continue to reach out to them.

COSMETIC CHRISTIANITY

It's easy for us to simply say, "Oh, these people just need to leave their lifestyles behind." But is it as obvious to know what *we* must do? Are there struggles or sins in *our* lives that hinder us from reaching out to others? Are we holding out on God?

Cosmetic Christianity is a plague within the body of Christ. It is a spirituality that is superficial and only skin-deep. Like the parable of the barren fig tree (see Luke 13:6–9), it promotes leaves—the appearance of spirituality—but it fails to produce the fruit and the character of Christ. Some cosmetic Christians actually have a relationship with the Lord, but some serious pruning is needed in their lives.

> *Cosmetic Christianity is a plague within the body of Christ. It is a spirituality that is superficial and only skin-deep.*

We are entering a season when we can no longer get away with things that are not pleasing to God. *Anything in our lives that is not like Christ must go!*

Even as Christians, we may try to cover up our hurts, fears, insecurities, and weaknesses through various kinds of compensatory façades. Such masks are an attempt to atone for something on the outside that we lack on the inside. The guise can be something "spiritual," such as Christian service, or it can be a worldly cover-up such as drugs, alcohol, promiscuity, or even material success. Whether the mask is spiritual or worldly, it will not bring true fulfillment. Our freedom comes only as we are open and transparent before the Lord.

DIGGING OUT THE ROCKS

Several years ago, I served on a missions team in Central America. We were helping a Youth With A Mission (YWAM) base that was working in a local village. One of our assignments was to help in the digging of an outhouse hole. I dug several feet down and hit a boulder. I soon realized that I could not get past this large rock, hard as I tried. The only way I could remove the boulder was to dig around it until I could get leverage to hoist it out of the hole.

Through that arduous process, the Lord spoke to my heart. Often our hearts contain hard rocks or boulders that block our spiritual progress. The Lord has to dig in our hearts, chipping away at any areas of hardness to pull out those boulders. There is no shame in willingly exposing ourselves before the Lord, because He knows and cares for us.

The enemy is cunning, and he knows how to appeal to our flesh. His tactics are no different today than the ones he used on Adam and Eve in the garden:

For God knows that in the day you eat of it [the forbidden fruit] your eyes will be opened, and you will be like God, knowing good and evil.   (Genesis 3:5)

With such enticing words, the enemy tries to draw us into his web. His temptation looks good and seems pleasant and desirable. Why is it that our human nature always seems to want what it cannot have? This was the initial temptation presented to Adam and Eve.

As soon as they ate from the Tree of Knowledge of Good and Evil, their eyes were opened. They now saw things from the world's standards. In the garden, Adam and Eve had *"the peace of God, which surpasses all understanding"* (Philippians 4:7), joy unspeakable, and everything good. The only thing they lacked or had to gain was evil. Yet the very thing they did not have, they desired.

When we believe the lies of the enemy that we *must be something* we are not, or *have something* we don't, we are no longer content being who we are in Christ. Believing a lie brings shame, and in our distress, rather than running *to* the Lord, we run *from* Him.

TRANSPARENT BEFORE THE LORD AND EACH OTHER

After eating the forbidden fruit, Adam and Eve experienced shame so they covered themselves and hid.

> *Then the eyes of both of them were opened, and they knew that they were naked; and they sewed fig leaves together and made themselves coverings....Then the LORD God called to Adam and said to him, "Where are you?" So he said, "I heard Your voice in the garden, and I was afraid because I was naked; and I hid myself."* (Genesis 3:7, 9–10)

Who told Adam he was naked? Who told *you* that you were naked? Who brings shame, fear of rejection, and lies into our lives?

What standard have we set for ourselves other than God's truth?

Being open and totally transparent before the Lord was Adam and Eve's original state—and it is our opportunity today. God knows everything about us already, so there is nothing to fear. We may be tempted by things in this world that seem good and pleasant, but if those things become our standard, we will no longer have peace in being transparent before the Lord.

> *We may be tempted by things in this world that seem good and pleasant, but if those things become our standard, we will no longer have peace in being transparent before the Lord.*

God wants us to look to Him and be content in Him. Our standard must be based on His purity, holiness, and righteousness, even if we don't think we can fit this standard. *It's better to try to fit His standards than to bring His standards down to ours.* This generation wants what is real and they are examining our lifestyle to see if we are authentic. We must allow the Lord access to those places of our hearts that we've tried to hide from Him. He sees them anyway! He wants only our good because He loves us. We lost our innocence in the garden, but Jesus gave it back at the cross! That is our hope and our victory.

Being right with God comes with a price, and that is our willingness to take off the masks, remove the façades and cover-ups, and let Him do a work inside us. God is not looking for those who merely *look like* Christians. He is looking for those who are the real deal. He wants believers who are the same inside and out. When we are transparent before the Lord, His light shines upon us and we radiate the very character and nature of His Son. That is what He is looking for and what the world hopes we have to offer—truth, honesty, and brokenness.

HUNGER FOR HOLINESS

Revival and holiness are synonymous. Revival is always first a revival of holiness and consecration. God is depositing a depth of character and a hunger for His holiness in each one of us who seek Him. As one Youth With a Mission leader stated about the Lord's work in Houston, "It is a revival of character."

The Lord wants to build a depth of character in our lives so that the move of His Spirit among us is not shallow and narrow, but deep and wide. For that to happen, we have to allow the Lord to uproot the old so that we can put on the new. When Jesus told His disciples that a grain seed had to die in order to bear fruit, He was speaking about Himself and us as well. (See John 12:24.)

During the Passover season in biblical times, the priest would take grains of wheat and scatter them in a field outside the city. He would then come back into the temple and sacrifice a lamb for the Passover. A pivotal year in history came when Jesus and the

Passover lamb of the temple were sacrificed at the same time. On the following Sunday morning before sunrise, the priest who had scattered the grains of wheat went out to see if they had sprouted. If so, he pulled up a few sprouts and brought these firstfruits into the temple to offer them on the altar.

At the same time as the sprouts were offered, Jesus, the first-fruit of the resurrection, arose. The grain of wheat had gone into the ground and died. Jesus had been buried, but on the third day, He arose.

Every time we make a sacrifice for His kingdom, we die to the flesh and God is glorified. From that place of sacrifice and death comes great fruitfulness and harvest. Death to self results in resurrection and multiplication. From our sacrifice, God will raise up what He desires in our lives. Though we may think we have little to offer, if we will offer ourselves, the Lord will produce a surprising fruitfulness. Jesus is returning for a church that has sown her life into the lives of others.

> *Though we may think we have little to offer, if we will offer ourselves, the Lord will produce a surprising fruitfulness.*

CAN WE HEAR THEM?

One day, as I met with a pastor and his wife, my cell phone rang. They waited politely, assuming that I was talking with my office or another minister. When I ended the call, the pastor asked, "Doug, who was that?"

"A crack addict," I replied. "He just needed some encouragement on how to seek the Lord. He hasn't broken his addiction yet, but I believe he's going to make it."

They sat quietly for a moment. Then the teary-eyed wife spoke. "Your heart has never changed," she said. "You still take the time to minister one-on-one. It's the same core DNA as you had back at that apartment years ago when you were trusting God for a bag of groceries."

Let us never arrive at a point where we no longer hear the cries of people's hearts. Let us not be so caught up in church life with the masses that we no longer have time for individuals ravaged by sin. Let's stop being in such a hurry to get to a choir practice or a prayer meeting that we pass all the needy on the street without so much as a whispered prayer for them.

An alarm is going off around the world. It's time for the church to arise and beckon people to enter the kingdom. We have been sent on a rescue mission to the multitudes by becoming a mended net cast into the waters to bring in a mighty harvest of souls.

Some say they want to impact the world, but they never seem to get started. Others claim that the challenges are just too great. Making an impact is actually a fairly simple task. *It's all about meeting real people, who have real needs, with the reality of Jesus.*

SOULS AT THE CROSSROADS

The life of Brandy, the young prostitute I mentioned earlier, illustrates the crossroads faced by every lost person today. Who will point them to Christ? Who will patiently help them, instruct them, and plant the seeds of eternal life in them?

Even though we worked with Brandy for years, she continued to struggle with her sinful lifestyle, ultimately dying of AIDS. Susie Wolf called all over the city the day Brandy died, but could not locate a single person who would claim to be related to the girl. Without next of kin, the county would have no recourse but to bury Brandy as an indigent in a pauper's grave.

But Brandy did have family. She had us. We would claim Brandy. We would mourn for her as one of our own. After a series of calls were made, I discovered that we could claim Brandy and give her a proper funeral for $2,500. I quickly gathered a small group and together we viewed a brief video clip of Brandy. Everyone agreed to help.

On the day of the funeral, local ministers, including Fred Forshag, George Matranga, Henry Dibrell, and Mark LeCrone, assisted with the service. Mark pastored a church in the Lower Westheimer area where we first met Brandy.

The local news media heard what we were doing and came out to ask why. At the service, strippers, street kids, and AIDS victims mixed with hospice workers and Somebody Cares staff. A young man we've known for over fifteen years had lived on the streets at the same time as Brandy. They stayed up many nights talking about their lives until he left the streets and entered a men's discipleship program. He said Brandy was "a big sister who looked out for me. She even took the blame for some things I did out there."

Brandy touched many lives. Among those attending the service was Lori, whom I'd met years earlier as she stood over her children's stroller while waiting to turn a trick. She, too, had contracted AIDS. During the service, she shared a few words about Brandy, then turned and pointed at me and said, "I wish I'd never left. I wish I'd listened to you back then."

> *The apostle Paul was often rejected, even persecuted and beaten, yet he helped win to Christ almost half the known world of his day.*

What will the people of your city say as they point a finger at you? Will they say they wished they had listened to you...or will they ask why you never told them? Each of us is vital to the lives of those we meet. We could be the only family these people will ever know. There *is* hope for the world. There is hope for young men and women just like Brandy, who are out on the streets today. Their hope is found in you and me. We are a tangible expression of Jesus's love for them.

The apostle Paul was often rejected, even persecuted and beaten, yet he helped win to Christ almost half the known world of his day. Listen to his joy at the work God did in his converts at Thessalonica:

> *What is our hope, or joy, or crown of rejoicing? Is it not even you in the presence of our Lord Jesus Christ at His coming? For you are our glory and joy.*   (1 Thessalonians 2:19–20)

This same joy can be ours as we unite to reach out to lost and hurting people with the power of the gospel. Will we continue on the road of complacency or press on down the road toward revival? Will we build our own kingdoms or join together to build God's kingdom? Never before have we been given such incredible opportunities to reach our cities for Christ. We have this amazing hour in which to fulfill our destiny. We must let nothing deter, distract, or discourage us. We must act now.

IS THE SAFETY NET READY?

When I think of all the people whose souls are hanging in the balance of an eternity without God, I am reminded of the tragic story of the *Titanic*. In stark contrast to Noah, who by divine warning obeyed God and built an ark to save his family (see Genesis 6–9), those who worked on the passenger liner *Titanic* arrogantly said that even God Himself couldn't sink her.

Six warnings were sent to the *Titanic* before she hit the iceberg that sank her. Throughout the day, various ships, including the

Californian and the *Carpathia*, sent warnings of impending danger, yet all warnings were scorned, and the rest is history.

We can see a parallel between the fate of the *Titanic* and the fate of a people who choose to ignore God's warnings. The word *pride* could be used to describe the actions of the *Titanic's* crew, as pride can describe so many today who reject the warnings of the Lord. But there were also three other ships in the *Titanic* story that must not be overlooked.

The *Samson* was a ship that many did not hear about until years later. It was the closest ship to the sinking *Titanic* and could have aided in rescuing many of those who perished in the icy sea, yet it chose to leave the scene. The crew of the *Samson* was involved in the illegal hunting of seals, and because they were afraid of getting caught, they turned off their lights and sailed away, leaving more than 1,500 to die a horrific death.

How many professing Christians have rendered themselves ineffective in rescuing perishing souls? Due to the dark deeds of sin, some do nothing. They run away from, rather than toward, those who are shipwrecked in the sea of death.

The next closest ship, the *Californian*, was in an ice field less than twenty miles away from the *Titanic*. Earlier, the *Californian* had sent warnings to the luxury ocean liner about the danger of icebergs, only to be ignored. Although the *Californian* was not far away, it only proceeded toward the *Titanic* the next day, after the great ship had sunk. There may have been a bit of pride involved in their decision not to hasten. After all, they did try to warn the *Titanic*.

I wonder how many believers choose to do nothing to help rescue the perishing because they don't want to risk their own comfort?

I wonder how many believers choose to do nothing to help rescue the perishing because they don't want to risk their own comfort?

The third ship, the *Carpathia*, was nearly forty-eight miles away from the *Titanic*, but when they received the distress call, they immediately chose to go full speed ahead. They, too, had earlier warned the *Titanic*, and their warnings went unheeded. The fog was thick, making it dangerous for the *Carpathia* to maneuver past icebergs, but at the risk of their own lives and against all odds, her crew chose to rescue the perishing. They were able to save the lives of just over 700 people, while more than a thousand others froze to death in the icy sea. How many more could have been rescued had the *Samson* and the *Californian* assisted the rescue efforts?

Like the passengers on the *Titanic*, people today are cruising along in smug complacency, living in relative prosperity. But when calamity comes, will there be adequate lifeboats to handle shipwrecked victims?

> *Mending our nets is not just a nice idea to make us look spiritual; it is a matter of life and death to countless people.*

The church needs to prepare for such a day. Mending our nets is not just a nice idea to make us look spiritual; it is a matter of life and death to the countless people who will drown when their lives strike an unexpected iceberg. In that day, the mended net will be a safety net to rescue lives for the kingdom. If our government welfare net were to rip open, would the church be ready to provide a network of food and clothing distributions to accommodate millions of people as we did in previous decades before government welfare? The answer is *yes* if the church unites now. By uniting in a similar way to the Somebody Cares network, we can position ourselves and prepare for the latter rain, the shaking, and the fires of revival. The fire will burn, the wind will blow, and the rain will fall, but the effect they have on us individually and corporately will depend on what we have done to prepare.

DEEP AND WIDE

Prior to one of the presidential elections, I was asked to speak at a large political convention. I would have spoken the same words regardless of which political party I was addressing. Little did I realize those words would resound and reverberate across America in what I believe is a prophetic word to the nation.

The following paragraphs, ending in a prayer modeled after a passage from Isaiah 37:15–20, are the gist of what I said that day:

> Everywhere I go today, I hear young people say, "Give me something to believe in." Hundreds of years ago, Hezekiah, a great national leader, said, *"This day is a day of trouble and rebuke and blasphemy; for the children have come to birth, but there is no strength to bring them forth"* (Isaiah 37:3). Today's generation of young people are looking for something to believe in. They are ready to be released into their destiny, but they need hope to bring that destiny to life. What we need in America again is hope.
>
> My prayer and my heart's cry is that our words would come from the innermost part of our hearts and not be just shallow platitudes or façades that compensate for a lack on the inside. I pray that we would help give strength to this generation that is ready to put their hope in something. They need to see a revival of character. They need to see a revival of trust in those who say they are leading them into the next century—the next millennium....

My prayer is that America would be a nation of hope once again...a nation of character...a nation in which all people can trust us...a nation in which this young generation will find their hope again and the outcast, the lame, and the sick will be a strong nation.

Lord God, You alone are God. Incline your ear to hear and open your eyes to see the distress and trouble, despair and hopelessness we see in the inner cities of America and all across this nation and around the world. We recognize that our shallow words and platitudes and our own efforts alone cannot bring change. We need your intervention. We need a revival of character....

Give a release to this young generation looking for something to believe in. Give them hope again. And, Father, release them to their destiny to walk in character, integrity and in the hope that they would lead us across the Jordan to a place of promise where the world can look to us and say they want some of that. Incline your ear, O Lord, and hear. Open Your eyes, O Lord, and see. Intervene on our behalf and make us a great nation again. In Jesus's name. Amen.

TO THE ENDS OF THE EARTH

When we see that what God has called us to do is too big for us, we will finally be ready for God to use us. One of our board members, Pastor Paul Tan of City Blessings Churches, was feeling overwhelmed one day as he considered the huge responsibility of reaching cities for Christ. As he cried out to the Lord, Paul sensed the Lord saying, "If it's not too big for you, then you don't need Me!" Indeed, God will never give us a mission that we can accomplish without His help or the help of our brothers and sisters.

When we come together, seeking God's strategy and power, there will be amazing fruit. Onlookers will see something we never could have accomplished without the Lord and each other.

> *You shall be witnesses to Me in Jerusalem, and in all Judea*
> *and Samaria, and to the end of the earth.*   (Acts 1:8)

This is a blueprint for any ministry vision. We first reach our local communities, *our Jerusalem*. Then we reach other parts of the nation, *our Judea*. From there, we take the kingdom to neighboring countries, *our Samaria*, and then to the rest of the world, *"the end of the earth."* The same kingdom principles work everywhere.

As we faithfully follow the Lord, our fig trees will be full. Our nets will bring in a great catch without breaking. It is harvesttime, and from every seed that dies, we can expect a great crop. Many will be brought out of the valley of decision because true witnesses will have rescued their lives.

Just as the vineyard owner gave the keeper a season to nurture his fig tree, we have been given a window of opportunity to fulfill God's purposes for this generation. The darkness is growing darker and the light is getting lighter. *"Where sin abounded, grace abounded much more"* (Romans 5:20). Together we must commit ourselves to His purpose and prepare people for His coming. This is our privilege and our calling.

EXPANDING AND
SPREADING THE NET

*So they departed and went through the towns, preaching the
gospel and healing everywhere.*
—Luke 9:6

When we started our Somebody Cares Houston citywide
outreach campaign, we had no aspirations of becoming an international organization. We were just a handful of people with a
passion for God and compassion for souls, connecting with others

in our city who had like minds and like hearts. Our first official chapter outside of the greater Houston area was Somebody Cares Tampa Bay in June 1997. In response to growing interest from many of our existing relationships across the nation and around the globe, we formed Somebody Cares America and International.

WHAT IS SOMEBODY CARES?

Somebody Cares America and Somebody Cares International have become a coalition and network of organizations and churches impacting communities through prayer initiatives, compassion outreaches, training, and responding in times of crisis, as well as encouraging and equipping leaders globally.

From Houston, Texas, to the four corners of the world, from urban to foreign missions, and from inner cities to unreached people groups, we are impacting communities and helping to transform lives through united efforts of prayer, tangible expressions of Christ, and community transformations through king-dom collaborations.

We have seen chapters, centers, and partner ministries and organizations launched across the nation and internationally, along with other ministries birthed from the Somebody Cares DNA. While they may look different—because the needs and the dynamics in their communities *are* different—many have gleaned from and incorporated the basic tenets of the Somebody Cares blueprint. By using the principles in this book, the influence of the *net that works* has expanded throughout cities, communities, and nations around the world.

Marlene Yeo started Somebody Cares New England (SCNE) to reach the homeless and underserved in her community of Haverhill, Massachusetts. The services they offer include assistance to the elderly, a monthly food pantry, emergency relief for grocer-ies and personal care, block parties, Thanksgiving groceries, and

Christmas gifts for children in need. Recently, SCNE expanded its outreach with the opening of Renaissance Worship Center, located on the campus of North Point Bible College and targeting the college and career, creative, performing arts, and entrepreneurial communities. Marlene serves on several civic committees and has been recognized on multiple occasions by state and local leaders for the work of SCNE.

Our Somebody Cares chapter in Baltimore serves the city with intentional initiatives to bridge the gap between residents, law enforcement, and the business community. Nearly 150 chaplains have been trained and deployed to ride with and support on-duty officers. Church leaders do regular prayer walks throughout the city. And thousands of community members come to the annual Day of Hope celebrations held in two locations each year, providing food, fun, and access to social service vendors. SC Baltimore also provides services to the homeless, including an annual Christmas banquet, and recently implemented a training program for facilitators to lead trauma healing circles.

Working through Church in the City-Beth Abraham, Somebody Cares Denver works to eliminate homelessness by engaging the community, empowering individuals, and educating the public. The chapter serves meals with the Morning Manna program, offered multiple times a week; provides a food bank where visitors can grab as much free food as they need twice a week; and works with those in prison so they do not become homeless when they get out. "We created our organization because we believe that no one should live or die in homelessness," says Pastor Michael Walker, who leads SC Denver.

BIRTHED FROM DISASTER

Mark Roye and his wife Susie were leading Blood -N- Fire San Antonio when Mark connected with me in the early 2000s and began attending various Somebody Cares meetings and think tanks in Houston. When Hurricane Katrina hit in 2003, Mark became a field rep for Somebody Cares America as he, Susie, and their team spent over thirty days serving evacuees at the old Air Force base in San Antonio. They provided meals, supplies, and personal items, as well as a listening ear and plenty of love and encouragement. They also held daily church services.

A few weeks later, after Hurricane Rita struck southeast Texas, Mark hitched up his cooker and headed out to Bridge City, Texas, a town nearly destroyed by the storm.

"We set up in the midst of total darkness and were able to feed 500 people that first night because we had our smoker," he recalls. "We didn't even have any food with us, but people smelled the smoke and started bringing the food from their freezers because it was going to ruin. Our first meal that night was shrimp, redfish, steak, and elk. People just started bringing us stuff, and we started cooking it!

"When we were feeding the poorest people in that community, the president of the bank was in the same line. Our mission wasn't necessarily about preaching the gospel; it was about feeding the hungry, being a tangible expression of the gospel, and networking with people."

Today, Mark deploys with his cooker to nearly every Somebody Cares America disaster site to scout out a distribution location, assess the community's needs, and serve hot meals to residents and first responders. The ministry in San Antonio has been officially renamed Blood -N- Fire/Somebody Cares San Antonio.

Somebody Cares Picayune in Mississippi was born out of a relationship with Pastor Allen Hickman and Pastor Richard Hinojosa of Resurrection Life Church. (Richard now pastors in Brownsville, Texas.) In the aftermath of Hurricane Katrina, the relationship proved to be providential. Resurrection Life Church and Ministries already had relational equity in the community that has exponentially increased far beyond their community since then. Pastor Hickman and Resurrection Life have become a vital part of Somebody Cares America and have responded to many relief efforts across the nation

Similarly, our relationship with Rey Matos, pastor of Catacumba 5 in Puerto Rico, led to the immediate formation of Somebody Cares Puerto Rico when Hurricane Maria wreaked havoc on the island. Many agencies and organizations connected with Somebody Cares Puerto Rico and the church to bring desperately needed supplies, volunteers, and assistance in some of the hardest hit areas. Somebody Cares America and International were also able to connect medical supplies from partner organizations to SCPR. They now operate a medical clinic for the needy that is overseen by Dr. Ricardo Machado-Torres, a member of Catacumba 5 and a well-respected medical doctor.

Somebody Cares Jasper-Newton Counties, Texas, was already in place prior to hurricanes Katrina and Rita. Led by Pastor Charles and Beverly Burchett from First Baptist of Kirbyville, their connections with and leadership in the community proved invaluable during relief efforts. After Hurricane Harvey flooded the region in 2017, they formed and continue to lead the Jasper-Newton Long-Term Recovery Group (JNLTRG) to steward resources for rebuilding. When Somebody Cares was awarded several large grants for the region, we partnered with the JNLTRG to assist families with home repairs and other unmet needs. In three years, by leveraging relationships and coordinating volunteers, the JNLTRG repaired, restored, and rebuilt 500 homes.

NEVER TOO EARLY, NEVER TOO LATE!

John Clifton was already retired from a successful business career when he felt a tug to begin Somebody Cares St. Augustine after hearing a talk by Daniel Bernard from Somebody Cares

Tampa Bay. From 2007 through 2018, John coordinated annual CareFest events that mobilized 1,000 volunteers from thirty-four churches of different denominations for hundreds of service projects.

"I didn't play the first three quarters very well," John says, referring to his earlier life. "I was all about making money and living in a country club, driving luxury cars, and being on the golf course." But God had other plans for John.

The network of relationships built through CareFest led to the chapter's next assignment when John was asked to serve on the St. Johns County school district's unaccompanied youth advisory board, working with homeless students. The definition of a homeless student is a student of any age who lacks a fixed regular and adequate nighttime residence. These homeless students include a number of "unaccompanied youth"—high school students, ages sixteen through nineteen, who are likely to be living on the streets.

"These are kids who are trying to get an education under the worst possible conditions," John explains. "They could be couch surfing. They could be living in their car. They might be living with a relative who doesn't have legal custody of them. Or they might be in the woods—but they're in school. These kids are trying hard and they need us."

Today, through the work of Somebody Cares, all forty-four schools in the school district have a church partner they can turn to for spiritual and material needs. An annual Coats 4 Kids drive provides winter clothing for every homeless student in the district, and an annual college scholarship is awarded to a deserving student. The chapter also provides gift cards, pays school fees, and covers emergency expenses for needs such as food, shelter, and gas.

"The fourth quarter has been the best quarter," John concludes. "It's been extremely encouraging and rewarding to be able to help these kids who are part of the next generation. To be the hands and feet of Jesus and to change their lives is pretty humbling stuff."

K.J., on the other hand, was only five years old when he saw news reports about Hurricane Katrina. He was heartbroken for the children who lost all their toys in the flooding and began collecting toys from his room to give away. That small act of compassion led to a toy drive partnering with retail stores in his hometown of Omaha. Two semi-truckloads of brand new toys were collected and shipped to Somebody Cares hurricane relief sites, where they were distributed to evacuees from Katrina and Rita. This event also led to the formation of a nonprofit that for several years mobilized the Omaha community to help local children in need.

IT'S NOT ABOUT THE NAME

When people come to me with a dream in their hearts to see a Somebody Cares chapter in their community, I always tell them it doesn't matter if they call it *Somebody Cares*. We just want to help them do something!

I still remember when Jerry and Jana Lackey, then newlyweds, told me how the Lord had placed the beautiful people of Africa on their hearts. When they first went to Botswana on a mission trip in the mid-1980s, they knew they would be returning there.

"Our heart's cry was for God to send us where nobody else is willing to go, where it's not popular or glamorous," Jana says. In this area of Botswana, there were no paved roads, and the villages were only accessible by airplane or a four-wheel drive vehicle. The Lackeys founded Love Botswana Outreaches; by networking and collaborating with other organizations, they have grown into the largest non-governmental organization in the nation and have birthed many other organizations. Today, the government of Botswana comes to them for help in facilitating programs dealing with issues such as children's rights, people with disabilities, and alcoholic families.

I've had the pleasure of being on Love Botswana Outreaches' board of directors for decades (and still am) and have personally seen the incredible grace upon their lives even through some of the most trying of times, including Jerry's battle with cancer. Jerry came to Houston for weeks of chemotherapy and was determined to get back to Botswana for their annual camp meeting for hundreds of pastors and leaders. So, literally, the day after his last chemo treatment in Houston, I flew with him to Botswana to make it just in time for their camp meeting. From the moment we arrived at the airport in Maun, many people greeted him warmly and affectionately. Over the years, when referring to the beautiful people of Botswana and Africa, he would do so with tears in his eyes. I can see why he is so well-received and loved.

Although the Lackeys don't use the name *Somebody Cares*, they have the same spiritual DNA. From the early days when I founded Turning Point Ministries International to the birthing of Somebody Cares America and Somebody Cares International later, they have also been a part of our global relationships.

"We want to be the hands and feet of Jesus, in our communities and in the villages," Jerry explains. "We want to show people what God's love looks like in practical ways. Somebody Cares has already modeled this."

The kingdom of God is built on relationships, first with God, then with one another. The degree of influence we have is determined by the level of those relationships. And when our relationships bring others into the kingdom, it doesn't matter who gets the credit, as long as God gets the glory.

Jerry confirms this when he says, "One of the keys to our success is that we came, through you, to understand that ministry is about relationships. We linked with people in the 1980s and

1990s that we are still associated with. Those relationships have stood the test of time because they were built on the essence of what we're trying to accomplish in the bigger picture of what God has called us to do."

PICK YOUR PASSION!

There are many others who have gleaned from the message of Somebody Cares and stepped out to follow their passions.

I remember when, after a weekly Bible study in my apartment, Dr. Stuart Quartemont pulled me outside to share what the Lord had put in his heart for medical missions. It was around 1986, and he was in residency at Southwest Memorial Hospital. Choked up and in tears, he told me the Lord had put it on his heart to go to Nigeria as a medical doctor after he completed his residency. He and his wife Velvet did just that.

From 1988 through 1991, they were missionaries in Nigeria, establishing medical clinics and schools. In 1991, they officially established Medical Mission International. Dr. Quartemont, a very respected physician in the Brazos Valley area of Texas, still goes on numerous trips to Nigeria and other nations. They have been an important part of the history and relationship with us at Somebody Cares International.

The Quartemonts are also part of our Somebody Cares Brazos Valley network, along with our longtime friends at S.O.S. Ministries in Bryan/College Station. Founded by J.J. Ramirez, S.O.S. is reaching hundreds through gang and at-risk youth intervention as well as homes for men and women.

Mike and Mandy Reiszner were well respected youth pastors who came to me for advice when they felt God leading them to work with orphans. They had no idea where to begin, so I recommended they join up with a Somebody Cares team that was leaving for Haiti after the devastating earthquake of 2010. That trip not only changed their lives but birthed CoreLuv, a ministry that has, in turn, changed the lives and destinies of hundreds of orphans while also offering internships to young people with a desire to serve. We are so blessed by the partnership with Mike and Mandy, and the ministry of CoreLuv, in reaching so many in need.

Mike Rosas, a minister, marketplace entrepreneur, and chaplain for the Houston Rockets, also founded an orphanage and poverty eradication initiative called Love Bought, working with orphans in Columbia.

Years ago, after I spoke at a dinner meeting for young leaders, Mike and Lidiette Rosas asked me to be a mentor and spiritual father to them. It's been encouraging to see all the Lord is doing in and through them over the years. We are honored to be a small part of their journey.

Kathy Alex, who served on our staff after she connected with us during Houston Prayer Mountain in 1996, was an integral part of our Somebody Cares Houston outreaches and beyond. She became a daughter in the ministry. A few years ago, she sensed a calling to return to her hometown of Lafayette, Louisiana, and took the Somebody Cares DNA with her. The Lord has used that DNA and Kathy's passion for her community as she has serves as chaplain with the Lafayette Sheriff's Department. She networks with local churches and agencies to bring healing and restoration to the hundreds of men and women who are incarcerated there.

Susie Wolf also served on our staff for many years and is still an integral part of the work we are doing as an ambassador of Turning Point Ministries International and Somebody Cares Houston. For many years, she was a caregiver for her elderly father, whom she also led to the Lord, and she developed a deep love for the elderly and an understanding of the need for advocacy. She is now founder and president of Seniority Services, Inc., with a mission to enhance the quality of life of the chronically ill, seasoned citizens, and their caregivers.

PRAYER WITH A PURPOSE

Gideon Stanley grew up in a praying family. In fact, his father, Simon, is recognized as a father of all-night prayer gatherings in India. Gideon and his wife Sara combined their passion for prayer with their heart for young people and founded iPray On Campus with a goal to mobilize students to pray in their schools. The Stanleys also operate a software company, with employees in the U.S. and India.

"Somebody Cares is restoring the church to its rightful posture of being the hands and feet of Jesus," Gideon says. "The Somebody Cares network is an embodiment of a network that demonstrates this principle in times of need and uncertainty." The Stanleys pray passionately for America and have mobilized young people to do the same.

There are so many amazing people and ministries that we've had the pleasure of partnering with and serving. Many of them have been a part of our Somebody Cares transformation training and intensives, as well as our Leadership Awakening intensives. They understand the importance of undergirding compassion outreach with prayer and action.

Calvin and Helen Miller are founders of 1 Team, 1 Fight, a ministry that includes prayer marches targeting gang violence, high crime, and sex trafficking. Some prayer marches have been in partnership with the police department and have been followed by lower crime rates, through the power of prayer.

Pastors Donnell and Stephanie Vigers of Church on Fire have helped to facilitate and served at gatherings in the greater Houston area, including a Reinhard Bonnke crusade in early 2015 and, most recently, Revival 4 Survival, a day of prayer and worship at Skeeter Baseball Stadium in Sugarland, just outside of Houston. Thousands attended locally and online, and Internet broadcasts reached nations all around the globe.

Donnell and Stephanie have participated in our various initiatives and I'm blessed to see how they have carried the message of *Mending the Net*, prayer, and compassion outreach in all they do. I often chuckle when Donnell tells people that Doug Stringer is the spiritual muscle in the region. I think it's just a nice way of saying that I have been around a long time!

ACROSS THE SEA

Over in the United Kingdom, Jenny and Brian Taylor stepped out with faith and a desire to *rescue lives* in their hometown of Aberdeen, Scotland, after being inspired by Somebody Cares Houston. Pockets of desperate poverty and pain marked their prosperous city in a way that broke their heart. As Somebody Cares Aberdeen was birthed they made a commitment:

Where there is need…to meet the need.

Where hope is gone…to help restore hope.

Where love is needed…to demonstrate love.

Beginning with a small warehouse, the Taylors began to meet others' needs. Today, they operate a 20,000-square-foot distribution center that refills as quickly as they give out! It has become one of the largest and most reputable outreaches in the region.

Far more important than the size of their building or number of giveaways are the lives turned around by their love and care. From international students to blue collar workers, from unemployed families to abandoned moms, Jenny, Brian, and the Somebody Cares network have been *true witnesses* to thousands.

Somebody Cares has also collaborated with partners in Fiji, Japan, the Caribbean, Brazil, Indonesia, and other places around the globe during times of disaster or ongoing crisis.

WHERE DO WE FIT?

Buddy and Carolyn Hicks left a stable job pastoring a large church in Humble, Texas, to start a ministry to young people, with the help of their daughter and son-in-law, Mike and Shari May. The new ministry included a skate park, a music venue outreach, a church, and a community center.

Buddy—who is now with Jesus—and Carolyn had been friends for years, as they had been sowing into the next generation in Houston and other locations throughout the Jesus Movement and beyond. When they stepped into this new venture, they aligned more intentionally with Somebody Cares to become Somebody Cares Humble.

"It was hard to know where we really fit," Mike says. "We were running a thriving outreach to the youth of our community. Were we a church? Were we a business? As significant as the impact of these ministries were, what we were doing was so unique it often felt like we were running alone. Who could relate to the challenges we were facing? Was there anyone we could look to learn from?"

Mike found connection and support through relationships he made through our Somebody Cares meetings, especially young leaders who were part of the Revolution Network gatherings—hosted by another son of the ministry, Pastor Mike Salazar—as well as some of our chapter leaders who were also reaching out to youth. Today, Mike is a vital part of our disaster response network as he documents needs and testimonies from our relief sites on video. Many of the video documentaries and footage from the tsunamis in Indonesia and Japan as well as hurricanes Katrina, Rita, Ike, and, most recently, Harvey and Laura, were filmed and put together by Mike.

I could tell you many other wonderful stories and testimonies like these. There is so much good news to share in the midst of so much negative news in the world today!

LOOK UP!

I'd like to leave you with some final thoughts, especially when there are so many experiencing stress, anxiety, and even fear over the seeming uncertainties in their lives. During troubled times, I like to share this Word from Jesus:

> *They will lay their hands on you and persecute you....But it will turn out for you as an occasion* [or opportunity] *for testimony.*　　　　　　　　　　　　(Luke 21:12–13)

Together, we have the opportunity to be *mending the net* and *bringing hope in a hurting world.* Let us not miss the windows of opportunity to *be* the gospel of good news. Rather than hiding away in our holy huddles, may we recognize that we can be a tangible expression of Christ to those around us, in our communities, cities, and nations.

> "My food," said Jesus, "is to do the will of him who sent me and to finish his work....I tell you, open your eyes and look at the fields! They are ripe for harvest."　　(John 4:34–35 NIV)

The only thing that can satisfy the longing in our hearts and souls is to do the will of God and to finish His work. To do so, we need to get our eyes off of our own two feet and look up. Look up and see the fields, ripe and ready! Look up from our circumstances and our situations and see the harvest! We are all called to be like the Good Samaritan, giving our time and resources to preach the gospel and heal the sick.

The harvest is out there, but as Leonard Ravenhill used to remind me, "The laborers are still too, too few." The only way to reach the world is for us to partner together in mending and casting the net.

> *They caught a great number of fish, and their net was breaking. So they signaled to their partners in the other boat to come and help them. And they came and filled both the boats, so that they began to sink.*   (Luke 5:6–7)

Like Jesus, we must find our satisfaction in doing the will of the Father. God has sent us *for such a time as this*. This is our moment! Let's mend the net so we can be the *net that works* and bring in a mighty harvest!

GO AND DO LIKEWISE

After He tells the lawyer the story of the Good Samaritan, Jesus asks this poignant question:

> *"So which of these three do you think was neighbor to him who fell among the thieves?" And he said, "He who showed mercy on him." Then Jesus said to him, "Go and do likewise."*
> (Luke 10:36–37)

Jesus is telling us here that we are all called to be Good Samaritans. We are called to reach out to a hurting world and show them God's mercy by being the tangible expression of Christ.

If we will *stay low* (in a posture of humility), *draw near* (stay close) to His presence, and *incline our ears to hear* what the Spirit of Lord is saying, we can be the bearers of *good news*.

If we are going to see lasting impact in our generation as the church, then we should first *be* the tangible expression of the gospel; be willing to *bring* the gospel of good news to so many who desperately need it; and have a passion to *broadcast* and proclaim good news in and through our lives. In a world of daily negative news, may we be the bearer of the eternal good news!

Be it, bring it, and broadcast it by the way you reflect and represent the Lord in your life.

> **Preach the kingdom of God...***preaching the gospel* [of good news] *and healing everywhere.*   (Luke 9:2, 6)

ABOUT SOMEBODY CARES

Somebody Cares operates in local communities across the U.S. and internationally, bringing hope by meeting the day-to-day needs of individuals in personal crisis and by mobilizing our existing network of ministries to respond to global tragedies.

Your ongoing prayers and support enable us to be the hands and feet of Jesus in the midst of daily physical, emotional, and spiritual needs in our communities, throughout the nation, and around the world.

Here's what two of my faith heroes, who have since gone to be with the Lord, said about Somebody Cares and the earlier book I wrote in 2001:

> This book is a refreshing guide to what happens when Christians choose to lock hands together and become a powerful force for reaching out to the people in their city. God has used Doug Stringer's inspiration and leadership to unify His body in Houston in order to win people to Christ. What is happening there is truly wonderful and unprecedented and is a model for other cities to follow.
>
> —*Bill Bright (1921–2003)*
> Founder, Campus Crusade for Christ, Orlando, FL

> Scripture tells us our care for and service to others is the measure of true greatness. And that is the testimony of Doug Stringer. To read this book is to know the heart of God and be touched by the Spirit of God.
>
> —*Edwin Louis Cole (1922–2002)*
> Founder, Christian Men's Network

Because Jesus cares, we care. And because you care, lives across the globe are impacted daily.

Thank you for caring!

For more information or a list of Somebody Cares chapters, contact:

Somebody Cares America
P.O. Box 925308
Houston, TX 77292-5308

713-621-1498

somebodycares@somebodycares.org

ABOUT THE AUTHOR

Doug Stringer is the founder of Somebody Cares America and Somebody Cares International, with chapters, centers, partners, affiliate ministries, and a global coalition and network of organizations and churches impacting communities through prayer initiatives, compassion outreaches, training, and responding in times of crisis, as well as encouraging and equipping leaders globally.

Doug is an internationally known author and communicator who speaks to thousands of leaders annually on topics such as compassion evangelism, persevering, courageous and transformational leadership, and community transformation.

With more than thirty-five years in ministry, he has visited numerous communities and nations. Doug has received recognition for the work of Somebody Cares both nationally and globally, including being named by *Charisma* magazine as one of the Top 12 Newsmakers of 2008 and by *Ministry Today* in 2014 as one of the 21 Most Influential Ministries of the 21st Century. As an American of Asian descent, he is considered a revivalist at heart, a bridge-builder, and an ambassador for Christ. During a gathering at the Lincoln Memorial in 2016, Doug was among a group of ministry leaders recognized by Dr. Alveda King, the late Bishop Harry Jackson, and others for their many years in the ministry of reconciliation.

Doug served on the Executive Leadership Committee for America For Jesus 2012 held in Philadelphia, Pennsylvania. In 2011, he served as the National Church Mobilization Coordinator and local host for The Response, with over 40,000 attendees in Houston, Texas. He has also helped to serve, facilitate, or coordinate similar types of Joel 2 and 2 Chronicles 7:14 Solemn Assemblies across the nation. Doug has served on the boards of many national and international organizations over the years, including the board of the One Star Foundation, appointed by the governor of Texas.

Among other works, Doug authored *It's Time to Cross the Jordan*; *The Fatherless Generation*; *Somebody Cares, a Guide to Living Out Your Faith*; *Born to Die...That We May Live*; *Hope for a Fatherless Generation*; *Living Life Well, the Spirit of the Commandments*; *In Search of a Father's Blessing*; and *Leadership Awakening: Foundational Principles for Lasting Success*. He was also a contributing author on *The Revival Study Bible* and other publications.

Welcome to Our House!

We Have a Special Gift for You

It is our privilege and pleasure to share in your love of Christian books. We are committed to bringing you authors and books that feed, challenge, and enrich your faith.

To show our appreciation, we invite you to sign up to receive a specially selected **Reader Appreciation Gift**, with our compliments. Just go to the Web address at the bottom of this page.

God bless you as you seek a deeper walk with Him!

WE HAVE A GIFT FOR YOU. VISIT:

whpub.me/nonfictionthx

WHITAKER
HOUSE